D1489254

Past praise for the work of Ann Marie Sabath

Business Etiquette:
101 Ways to Conduct Business With Charm and Savvy

"Assists individuals in enhancing their understanding of the 'perception impact.'"
—William H. Bagley, former regional director of
human resources, Deloitte & Touche

"Powerful and thought-provoking."
—John Daw, former vice president of
Field Sales, Marriott Lodging

"Anyone who wants to make a great impression on coworkers or customers can benefit from the tips provided in this book."
—Sheila Casserly, former president, Celebrity Focus

One Minute Manners

"*One Minute Manners* offers quick, practical answers to the everyday situations we face in the workplace. From mastering the handshake to avoiding e-mail gaffes, this book serves as a survival guide for senior managers and entry-level employees alike. More than just preventing a faux pas, Sabath illustrates how playing your cards right at work can actually help advance your career."
—Rod Kurtz, former senior editor, Inc.com

What Self-Made Millionaires Do That Most People Don't

52 Ways to Create Your Own Success

Ann Marie Sabath

The Career Press, Inc.

This edition first published in 2018 by Career Press, an imprint of

Red Wheel/Weiser, LLC
With offices at:
65 Parker Street, Suite 7
Newburyport, MA 01950
www.redwheelweiser.com
www.careerpress.com

ISBN: 978-1-63265-134-1
Library of Congress Cataloging-in-Publication Data

Library of Congress Control Number: 2018932272

Cover design by Howard Grossman/12E Design
Interior by Gina Schenck
Typeset in Minion Pro and Palatino Linotype

Printed in Canada
MAR
10 9 8 7 6 5 4 3 2 1

Acknowledgments

To Ron Fry, whose belief in serendipity believed in this book from the very beginning.

To my Ahuvi, who was the catalyst for this book and was supportive during the entire process.

To my children, Scott and Amber, who were great sounding boards as I wrote this book.

To Germaine, whose coffee table conversations made me recognize the need for this book.

To Suzy, who was instrumental in researching the self-made millionaires in this book and helping me to meet deadlines early.

To the thirty self-made millionaires who took time from their busy schedules to share their words of wisdom.

To my senior editor, Michael Pye, who is a true publishing gent.

To Laurie Kelly-Pye, who is a true pleasure to work with.

To Lauren Manoy, the developmental editor of Career Press, whose "take on the book" made it worth putting the rest of my life on hold to write it.

To Jodi Brandon, who was a pleasure to work with during the editorial process.

To Gina Schenck, whose attention to detail made the final editing process flawless.

To Tess Woods, my publicist, a true guru in her industry who did a phenomenal job.

To Bonni Hamilton and Eryn Eaton, who are part of the Red Wheel marketing team.

To Jane Hagaman, the managing editor of Red Wheel.

To Mike Conlon and Jeff Piasky in production, who gave the book "a face" and got it to the finish line.

Contents

Introduction

Who Should Read This Book? Everyone!

Perhaps the title, *What Self-Made Millionaires Do That Most People Don't,* grabbed your attention. If you are like most individuals, you work long hours and wonder what others do to become successful knowing that they have the same twenty-four hours in each day.

Becoming a self-made millionaire may sound like a daunting task. After you read this book, however, you will realize that it is not. The secret is discovering what to do and then *staying on course.*

You may be saying to yourself: *"I am twenty-five years old. I am only a few years into my career and I want to have fun. I just bought the car I have dreamed of owning since I was sixteen. I'll get serious about saving in ten years."*

Or you may be thinking: *"I have a family with kids to feed, bills to pay, and a big mortgage for our four-bedroom house. Unless I win the lottery or inherit money from a long-lost uncle, I will never become a millionaire."*

Or you may be saying: *"I have been in my career for twenty years. It is too late to start now. I take trips with the extra money that I have."*

Although you may need to delay instant gratification and re-prioritize your goals, recognize that the only thing keeping you from starting on this course is you! By being attracted to this book, it shows that you have a desire to achieve this status.

Why put off for tomorrow what you can begin doing today? Whether you are on straight commission, making an hourly wage of $11, or are between the ages of twenty and sixty-five and earn the median wage for U.S. workers of $44,564, start now! The sooner you begin this journey, the sooner you will achieve this status.

Please don't be fooled. This self-made millionaire quest may take you five, ten, twenty, thirty years, or longer to achieve. It depends on how many of the fifty-two secrets you already have in place as well as the financial foundation that you have for beginning your journey. So, set your self-made millionaire GPS directions and get started!

Some of the secrets for achieving self-made millionaire status have nothing to do with money. You will see that they have to do with your character, your attitude, your people skills, your saving and spending patterns, and your habits in general.

Do not let not having enough money keep you from beginning this trip. By starting today, you will be one day closer to achieving this goal. You will not have to live the life of a pauper. *Au contraire!* You will be living the life of a successful person because of the road map that you will have created for yourself. Just think how gratified you will feel along the way to know with certainty that you are moving in the right direction.

A Few Facts

Credit Suisse released its annual Global Wealth Report, which found that the United States had about 15,356,000 millionaires in 2017, which adds up to nearly 5 percent of the total U.S. population.[1] Sixty-seven percent of high-net-worth Americans are self-made millionaires according to a study by BMO Private Bank.[2]

According to Thomas Stanley, author of *The Millionaire Next Door*, between 80 and 86 percent of millionaires have created their own wealth.[3] That is precisely who this book is about: individuals who have become millionaires on their own!

These individuals with a two-comma net worth (to not include their primary residences) are considered middle class by today's socioeconomic standards. The reason that I made a point to ask these individuals to be part of this book is to let anyone and everyone know that *you* can do it, too!

You only need two things:

1. To **believe** that you can do it.
2. A **mastery** of the 52 Secrets for Creating Your Own Success.

Who Will You Meet in This Book?

If you are looking for celebrity millionaires, this is not the book for you. I intentionally chose to interview people who are "closet millionaires." In other words, these are people who do not scream "I made it!" based on what they wear, the car they drive, and where they live. These are ordinary people who created their wealth from scratch and to whom everyone can relate. They achieved millionaire status between the ages of sixteen and sixty-five.

Their backgrounds vary. They are first-, second-, and third-generation American men and women. They are white-collar professionals and blue-collar workers. They are nine-to-fivers who got up and went to work every day. You will also read about entrepreneurs who had a good idea and ran with it. The majority of the people you will read about are still active in their businesses.

You will read about a person who made it thanks to going against his mother's wishes, another individual who spent his life digging ditches before he started his fiber optics company, and a third person who at fifteen years old came to the United States with his parents not speaking English, carrying one suitcase and a violin. You also will meet an individual who is actually the "Chief Happiness Officer" at his company.

Some of these individuals started their own businesses. Others were dedicated employees in a corporate environment. Some even failed before succeeding. Others had no choice except to succeed in order to provide for their families. Others subconsciously loved the chase. No matter the reason, they all did whatever it took to achieve their definition of "success."

As you read this book, you will notice that some individuals have disclosed their full names. Others have been willing to share their stories but have requested to remain anonymous. In either case, I can guarantee that you will be inspired by their candidness.

Although these individuals did not know each other when interviewed for this book, they all have something in common: *the 52 Secrets for Creating Your Own Success.*

Preconceived Notions About Self-Made Millionaires

Self-made millionaires would have been much more recognizable if I had not had preconceived notions about them that were wrong.

I had read *The Millionaire Next Door* when it first hit bookstores in 1996. However, I still held the misconceptions that the self-made ones lived in the most expensive neighborhoods, drove the newest cars, and stood out in a crowd.

Only when I actually spent quality time with self-made millionaires did I realize that Thomas Stanley's findings were right and my beliefs were wrong.

Misconception: Self-made millionaires graduated from Ivy League schools.

Finding: Though some have, others graduated from public institutions. Some only have a high school education, and others did not finish high school.

Misconception: They drive the latest model car.

Finding: Only a small percentage of self-made millionaires do.

Misconception: Self-made millionaires do not worry about the amount of money they spend.

Finding: The majority of self-made millionaires live below their means. Some even fit the frugal category.

Misconception: Self-made millionaires dress in the most up-to-date fashions.

Finding: Although some wear updated fashions, the majority do not dress to impress. They wear classic, conservative clothing.

Misconception: Self-made millionaires have an air of being better than those of lower socioeconomic statuses.

Finding: The majority of self-made millionaires are humble and donate their time to their community and/or the charity of their choice.

Misconception: Self-made millionaires live in expensive' neighborhoods.

Finding: Many prefer not to flaunt their status and live in houses in the suburbs.

Misconception: Only certain personalities are cut out to achieve self-made millionaire status.

Finding: The most quiet to the most gregarious have achieved this success.

Misconception: You need a great concept to build a business.

Finding: You need a timely idea, a strong work ethic, and follow-through to build a successful business.

What These Self-Made Go-Getters Do Differently Than the Average Joe

The reason I wrote this section last is that I wanted to observe the differentiating factors between self-made millionaires and the average person. I indeed did as I got to know many of the thirty self-made millionaires interviewed for this book.

The answers were right before my eyes. I now see them clearly and would like to share them with you. Before I tell you what they are, let me tell you the qualities that you might *think* were the differentiators, are not in the slightest.

These successful individuals were *not* better educated than the average person. In fact, one of them did not even finish high school. The majority were not born into wealthy families. Most of them were born into families of middle-class or lower-middle-class incomes.

Hmmm. So if it is not an Ivy League education or a bank roll that got them started, what was it? The answer: They had what money cannot buy. They had and still have the intangible traits that everyone can acquire.

I have divided what these people do differently than the average person into eighteen areas for this section. What differentiates self-made millionaires from individuals who have not yet achieved this status is the way they think, their persevering "I know that I can do it" mindset, and their mastery and respect for time. Other traits that differentiate them is their positive attitude, their organizational skills, and their relationship with money. Most of all, their consistency and discipline have been instrumental in achieving the success they have today. Their success formula is the mastery of the fifty-two secrets and then remaining disciplined in order to maintain their seven-figure status.

Following are the eighteen qualities that these thirty individuals did and continue to do in their businesses and their personal life. You will see that with proper discipline and consistency, self-made millionaire status is within *your* reach. These individuals:

1. Create their own destinies.

2. Use their time wisely.

3. Have a high emotional quotient.

4. Are confident.

5. Are trustworthy.

6. Think "outside the box."

7. Recognize the value of simplicity.

8. Are creative.

9. Keep doing "it" until they succeed.

10. Do not let their success status inflate their egos.

11. Respect their bodies.

12. Enrich their minds.

13. Recognize that they are only as good as the people in their lives.

14. Have the right priorities.

15. Are givers rather than takers.

16. Plan for their futures.

17. Treat money with respect.

18. Are resourceful.

How Self-Made Millionaires Benefit From What Most People Call Failure

Did you know:

> ➤ Oprah was fired from her first news anchor job in Baltimore because of the heart and soul she invested in her stories?

> ➤ Thomas Edison was told by his teachers that he was incapable of learning?

> ➤ A movie executive told Harrison Ford he would not succeed in movies?

Self-made millionaires achieve their success status because of how they interpret outcomes. Whereas most people see unexpected outcomes as failures, self-made millionaires use these outcomes as launching pads for their next try.

Though it may sound like a paradox, self-made millionaires learn from their failures. They figure out what should have been done differently before returning to the batting cage. They do not have "failure" in their vocabulary.

Turning failure into opportunities is such an important attribute of successful people that it has been earmarked as the twentieth secret for creating your own success.

How to Make This Book Work for You

Make this book work for you by comparing and contrasting your success traits with those self-made millionaire secrets described in each section. You will have many "aha moments" when you recognize the qualities that are so obvious, yet you may not have put into practice.

Each of the fifty-two secrets ends with an action step. After reading the entire book, figure out which practices you already have mastered. Then each week, focus on one action that you have yet to master. The secrets that are new to you will be the ones that will take the most effort. They will also be the ones that will have the greatest impact and get you to the self-made millionaire finish line.

Habit 1

They Think Big

Secret 1 for Creating Your Own Success: Create a Millionaire Mindset

Becoming a self-made millionaire does not just happen. If it did, you would be one by now.

Individuals who have accomplished this wealth status begin with a different approach than most. They do what I call "reversal thinking." They begin with the end in mind.

Step One: Conceive!

These individuals who create a millionaire mindset begin by defining *exactly* what they want in very specific terms. In other words, they *conceive* it.

Sounds easy, doesn't it? It is!

Let's do a dry run: *Conceive* what you want by putting "reversal thinking" into practice. Let's say you have *conceived* that you want to be a self-made millionaire. One step down, two to go!

Step Two: Believe!

Believe it! Hmmmm. Do you *really* believe that you can become a self-made millionaire? Seriously, do you? Hopefully, these two questions made your convictions for wanting to be one even stronger.

If your mind flooded with all the reasons that you cannot become a millionaire, *write down every single one of them now.* ("I can hardly make ends meet. I have a car payment, I have a house payment. . . .")

Now, take your written words of doubt and shred them. Yes, tear them up with all your might. By doing so, you will be dispelling these doubts from your mind. Anytime a doubt creeps into your mind, repeat the process of writing it down and tearing it up!

Rather than allowing yourself to be plagued with naysayers who tell you that your self-made millionaire goal is just "pie in the sky" thinking, keep your *conceive* and *believe* convictions to yourself. As you keep reading this book, you will learn how to replace these negative people with individuals who will root you on to achieving what you want. In fact, Secret 27 (Surround Yourself With People You Want to Be Like) and Secret 28 (Find a Brain Trust Advisor) will be instrumental in maintaining your self-made millionaire mindset.

Step Three: Achieve!

Now write this down three times: I will *achieve* self-made millionaire status. I will *achieve* self-made millionaire status. I will *achieve* self-made millionaire status. Remember: Keep believing it with all your heart! Put one of your "I will achieve self-made millionaire status" notes under your mattress, another in your wallet, and the third one in the glove compartment of your car—

virtually anywhere that no else is likely to look except you. Also, keep this in the notes section of your phone.

You may now be asking: Fine, so I have *conceived* that I will become a self-made millionaire. I am revved up and I do *believe* that I can *achieve* this wealth status. I have no clue, however, how I should go about doing it.

Please realize that it is not the answer that you are looking for. Simply ask the question first: How will I accomplish becoming a self-made millionaire? I promise that it *will* come to you. It may take a few weeks, a month, a year, or even five years. Be patient and listen to yourself. The answer *will* come to you.

Guess what? You are on your way! I have successfully used this CBA (conceive, believe, achieve) strategy numerous times in my life for the past forty years, and I promise you that it *does* work.

Your self-made millionaire mindset will be based on what you keep between your ears: your thoughts. The thirty self-made millionaires in this book will show you through their first-hand experiences how they *achieved* this status.

As Andy Hidalgo, one of the self-made millionaires in this book, says, "You can do it. You just have to want it."

ACTION STEP: PUT YOUR MILLIONAIRE MINDSET INTO PRACTICE BY CONCEIVING, BELIEVING, AND ACHIEVING WHAT YOU WANT.

Secret 2 for Creating Your Own Success: Define What Success Means to You

How do you define success? Many people see it as having a goal and accomplishing it. Every day, you experience success on both a personal and a professional level. You make a list of what you want to accomplish before leaving for work and you successfully complete each item. You want to complete a project by the end of the day and you indeed do it.

All of these little achievements give you the confidence to prepare for greater successes. Recognize that the principle for accomplishing both big and small successes takes the same system: having a goal, setting a time line, and accomplishing it.

I found it rather surprising that some people are actually afraid of "success." Perhaps it is because they experienced a failure and, rather than learning from it and moving forward, they allowed the negative situation to paralyze them into believing that success is not within their reach.

Their mindset is much different from those individuals who have a positive connotation of success. Based on their past accomplishments, these individuals define this seven-letter word positively. In their minds, their experiences gave them the confidence and know-how for future "successes."

The goal of this book is for you to see that success is within your reach. It is up to you to define what you want and put the 52 Secrets for Creating Your Own Success into practice.

I asked the self-made millionaires interviewed for this book how they define success. Here's what a few of them said:

"Success is whatever makes you happy." —Connie L.

"Providing for my children, making a positive impact in my profession, achieving stretch goals that have positive benefits personally and professionally." —John Pierce

"Being happy with yourself and the man that you see in the mirror; not just when others are happy with you." —Mickey Redwine

"Being happy. Having balance in life, feeling fulfilled, loved, appreciated, and having the ability to take care of yourself, your family, and still have enough to help others." —Steve Humble

"Having people appreciate what you do, being happy, being able to relax, and having enough money to be secure enough that you don't have to get up or go to work every day to survive and still having people respect you." —James Timothy White

"Making money while doing something I love." —Mike Vetter

"Taking care of my family and being able to help others in need." —Bunny Lightsey

"Winning in your chosen craft." —Nick Kovacevich

"Making enough money in doing what I love. Creating a legacy that will live on." —Tom Corley

"The ability to do things that make me happy without fear of monetary or other professional stress." —Bill Dunn

"Doing what you love and enjoying it." —Allan S.

"Achieving your personal wealth goals while never compromising your integrity or family values." —Andy Hidalgo

"Having an ongoing connection with your inner being." —Dr. Zach Berk

"If you can learn from your failures without losing enthusiasm and are liked and respected by others, you have found success." —Rodger DeRose

"Being successful is something that is accomplished when a passion of mine is pursued and its end result is received well by individuals who I also admire." —John M.

Three Ways to Define Your Own Success

1. Write down the last project that you started and successfully completed.

2. Document the process that it took to complete the above project.

3. Explain the benefits you experienced as a result of accomplishing it.

ACTION STEP: DOCUMENT YOUR DEFINITION OF SUCCESS.

Habit 2

They Know They Have to Believe "It" to See "It"

Secret 3 for Creating Your Own Success: Find Your Passion

Do you spend your working day doing what you love or dreading it? If you love what you do and are good at it, then you have found your passion. If you are trying to figure it out, this is an important secret for you!

Let me give you my passion: I love telling people what to do. I don't mean bossing them around. I mean guiding them to be successful. That's why I began my thirty-one-year-old corporate training business—to train young professionals how to climb that slippery ladder of success.

Your turn. Let's find your passion. What do you like to do or read about in *your* spare time? Do you like to exercise, travel, or write? Or perhaps you enjoy watching those real estate fixer-upper shows, or love antique hunting or traveling? The first step to finding your passion is to figure out what you enjoy doing so much that hours pass without you even realizing it. Once you have figured that out, you will have found your passion!

Many people are bogged down with doing what they don't like. Besides being miserable, they make everyone else's life around them unpleasant. Does that describe you?

Let me tell you about Allan S., the first self-made millionaire who you will meet in this book. Although he may not have known it immediately, Allan found his passion on his ninth birthday when his parents bought him a violin.

At first, Allan practiced like most kids who take lessons: thirty minutes a day. After a few years, he did not have to be told to practice. In fact, he enjoyed playing the violin so much that he chose to practice an hour a day and eventually four hours a day! Now if that is not finding your passion, what is?

When it was time to choose a course of study, Allan's mom urged him to study medicine or law. Not on Allan's list. He went against his mother's wishes and applied to the Juilliard School of Music.

During his time at Juilliard, Allan met a master violinist who asked to hear him play. The professional violinist told Allan that he played well however he should choose another profession, because being a musician was a difficult career path.

Luckily, Allan's gut and passion for playing the violin reigned supreme. He continued to practice four hours a day. He even auditioned for a position with a world-renowned symphony orchestra and was not selected.

Rejection did not discourage Allan from following his passion. He continued to practice and two years later auditioned once again for the open violin position with the New York Philharmonic. That time he was offered the position by Leonard Bernstein!

Allan spent his thirty-five-year career with the New York Philharmonic. This is what happens when you follow your passion!

After you find your passion, you have to stick with it. In Allan's case, it did not just happen. It took 1,600 hours of practice over a sixteen-year period. It took going against others' wishes by continuing to follow his passion rather than to take a career path that others believed would be better for him.

Now it's your turn to find your passion by following this three-step approach:

Step One: Find your passion. Take your time to figure it out. It may be right before your eyes. You will recognize your passion when it comes to you.

Step Two: Monetize it. Once you find your passion, talk to people who have the mutual interest in what you love doing. Find out how they turned it into a revenue stream. This will help you to figure out what it is going to take to build an enterprise around your identified passion.

Step Three: Stay on course. Avoid getting discouraged when naysayers tell you that you are wasting your time. Instead, follow your burning passion and overcome obstacles along the way.

ACTION STEP: FIGURE OUT WHAT YOU LOVE DOING THAT YOU CAN MONETIZE.

Secret 4 for Creating Your Own Success: Believe in Yourself

If a high IQ made people successful, only those who excelled in school would lead. If money alone made people successful, only the wealthy would have created today's inventions. Although a high intellectual quotient and money are good to have, neither is one of the fifty-two secrets for creating your own success. What *is* one of the essential secrets is *believing in yourself.*

Dropping out of college is certainly not a condoned action, though many successful people did it. That includes Oprah Winfrey, Mark Zuckerberg, Brad Pitt, Ted Turner, Steve Jobs, and the list goes on. What these moguls had in common was believing in themselves.

Think about the very smart people you know. They may have great ideas, yet do not have enough self-confidence to take their concepts to that next level. Also, give thought to those individuals who were far from rocket scientists but believed in themselves enough to create a million-dollar company out of a simple concept.

The difference between these two types of individuals is that those who were less confident convinced themselves that their idea would not be successful while the more confident people did not think twice about their ideas not working. In fact, what sold their concepts to others was first their belief in themselves *and* what they had conceived.

Which one are you? The person without confidence who talks yourself out of things? Or the one whose confidence is so contagious that you convince others about your idea through your belief?

Let me introduce you to Laura FitzGerald, the second self-made millionaire in this book. Laura believed in herself enough to achieve her millionaire status at the age of fifty-one. She is a terrific example of what the magic of believing can do. Laura believed in herself enough to become both the president of Ilios Resources and a Professional Certified Landsman. She founded her Shreveport, Louisiana–based company, which is an active buyer of minerals in North Louisiana, East Texas, and South Arkansas.

Laura is often quoted as saying, "I've made others millions of dollars. I can make you millions, too." When asked how *the magic of believing* in herself and her business guided her to be the success that she is today, Laura explained that it was with tireless and relentless study and learning, and continuing to try again, that she learned to believe in herself and never give up. Many times, the only way Laura has been able to explain or describe that "magic of believing" was through God working in her life.

Note: Laura plays a "man's game" for a living as a "land and mineral rights person." She finds, buys, sells, brokers, and leases land for mineral rights (oil and gas). Since 2004, Laura has accumulated more than 40,000 acres of mineral rights, which has made her millions. If that is not believing in yourself, what is?

John M., the third self-made millionaire interviewed for this book, made his first million at the age of seventeen. He says, "You must believe in yourself more than anyone else. No matter what age you are or what background you come from, no one will champion your pursuits more than you."

Three Ways to Muster Up Belief in Yourself

1. Be a "can do" rather than a "can't do" person. When a negative thought enters your mind, reverse it with a positive phrase. Example: Change "I am too tired to go to the gym" to "I will muster up the energy to work out for thirty minutes."

2. When you come up with what you consider to be a great idea, read about others who have turned their ideas into realities. This will build your confidence to develop your idea and, in time, make it real.

3. Read, listen to, and surround yourself with positive words and people. Recognize that you are the sum of the four people with whom you spend the most time.

ACTION STEP: CONVERT AN IDEA THAT YOU HAVE BEEN PONDERING INTO A REALITY.

Secret 5 for Creating Your Own Success: Visualize

Athletes use it. Homeopathic practitioners recommend it. Self-made millionaires do it.

You do it several times a day. You visualize an action within reach and then make it a reality.

Visualization is simple. Simply form mental pictures in your mind and then go through the process of making what you want a reality. The stronger your character, the sooner (weeks, months, years) what you visualize will come to fruition.

You may be asking, "If it is within everyone's reach, why is it that so few people practice it?" If you are one of those individuals who have not yet integrated this magical process into your life, then let me give you three case-in-point examples about how the visualization process works.

Tom Corley's Visualization Practice

Tom Corley, the fourth self-made millionaire interviewed for this book, explained to me that he uses a three-step process for making his dreams a reality. First, he *defines* his dream. Second, he *defines the goals* behind his dream. Third, he *actualizes* what he wants by *pursuing his goals every day.*

Step One: Define your dream. Tom *set the dream* of being on national TV.

Step Two: Define the goals behind your dream. Tom's goals were to share his *Rich Habits* research and to help promote his books.

Step Three: Pursue your goals every day. For three and a half years, Tom tweet-pitched the media close to 25,000 times in an effort to make that dream a reality.

Tom Corley's Dream Became a Reality

In June 2013 one of his tweets caught the eye of Farnoosh Torabi, host of Yahoo Finance's award-winning show *Financially Fit*. The interview was released on July 16, 2013, and received more than two million hits within a twenty-four-hour period. That got the attention of CBS, who asked Tom to travel to their Boston affiliate studio for an interview. The CBS interview was released in November 2013 by CBS's Boston affiliate. The interview was picked up by other affiliates in the United States and Canada. Tom was seen on *CBS Evening News* by more than ten million viewers. The result was that he sold thousands and thousands of books through his masterful art of visualization.

A well-deserved standing ovation for Tom. Visualization is easy when you follow the three-step process. You see, however, that it does not just happen.

Allan S. Visualization Law of Expectancy Practice: "Act As If"

You read about Allan S. in Secret 3 (Find Your Passion). Now let me tell you how this self-made millionaire used visualization to accomplish selling his house.

Allan and his wife bought their house after their first child was born. They raised both daughters in the house. Forty-eight years later, their daughters were married with families of their own. A few years after Allan's wife passed away, he was ready to sell the house that had been their home. However, it had not been renovated for more than half a century.

Rather than stressing out about it, he found a realtor and put it on the market. His thought was to give each of his daughters a lump sum from the house sale proceeds. One day after the "for sale" sign was placed in his yard, he "acted as if" he had sold it. He wrote a note to each of his two daughters describing how much he and their mom enjoyed raising them in what had been their home. Allan also wrote a check to each of them and post-dated the checks three months from the actual date that he had written the notes.

Two weeks later, Allan received an offer on his house. It looked like he may have had a little help from his best friend—his wife. Although deceased for four years, the offer for the sale of the house came in on July 14—her birthday. His "act as if" worked for him!

"Yeah, yeah, yeah," you may be thinking. If you are not yet convinced about the power of visualization, then keep reading.

My Personal Visualization Experience

When my first book, *Business Etiquette in Brief,* was released in 1992, I intentionally put one of the author copies on the top shelf of my dining room hutch. Next to it, I carefully placed Oprah Winfrey's book, *In the Kitchen With Rosie,* with their corners touching.

When my children returned home from school that afternoon, they noticed the books oddly placed in the hutch with our family crystal and sterling silver. They asked why I would do that. With all my heart, I explained to them that I was visualizing an invitation to be a guest on *The Oprah Winfrey Show*. Because my son and daughter did not yet understand the power of visualization, they thought I was crazy.

For four years Oprah's book and mine were best friends. They remained visible in our glass-enclosed dining room hutch that I would see every time I passed through the room.

During late autumn 1996, I was working from home on a weekly newspaper column deadline that was due later that day. I had asked my assistant, Suzy, not to call me unless it was absolutely essential. Around 2:00 p.m. that afternoon, the phone rang. Suzy said that I had to return a call that she had just taken. When I questioned her if it could wait until the following day, she insisted that I had to return the call immediately. She gave me the 312 area code followed by the telephone number and the name of the person. When I asked her the name of the company, she said, "Harpo Productions." I asked her what kind of company that was. Her answer: "Oprah spelled backward!" The call was from a producer of *The Oprah Winfrey Show* inviting me to be a guest on their show!

You ask how that happened? It is called visualization! My "doubting Thomas" children are now firm believers of this practice. I hope that you are, too!

Are you ready to make what you want a reality? Begin materializing it through the power of visualization.

> ➤ Define your dream. Make sure it is for the good of all.

> ➤ Document the goal behind your dream.

> ➤ Begin making your goal a reality by documenting it in clear terms and/or by finding a picture of what you want and placing it in a location that you see daily.

> ➤ "Act as if" it has already happened.

ACTION STEP: FIGURE OUT EXACTLY WHAT YOU WANT, WRITE IT DOWN, AND THEN "ACT AS IF" YOU HAVE RECEIVED IT.

Habit 3

They Are Intentional

Secret 6 for Creating Your Own Success: Set Meaningful Goals

In order to get where you want, you have to know where you want to be in the first place!

Let's say that you want to lose ten pounds, you want to start a business, *or* you want to become a self-made millionaire! Begin with the end in mind: *your goal.*

Here is what Joe Berry, investment advisor of the Semmax Financial Group, recommends:

> First, you need to pick a goal that is meaningful to you and that you will be willing to 'sacrifice' for when other temptations and needs arise. Second, you need to put your goals in writing and revisit them frequently so that you can stay focused on meeting your goal.[1]

Most people give thought to what they want and then focus on accomplishing it. They forget one important step: to write it down.

Mark McCormack's book, *What They Don't Teach You at Harvard Business School*, describes a study conducted on students in the 1979 Harvard MBA Program. That year, the students were asked, "How many have set clear-written goals for your future and made plans to accomplish them?" Surprisingly:

> ► Eighty-four percent of the individuals had no goals.

> ► Thirteen percent had goals that were *not* in writing.

> ► Only 3 percent of the graduates had committed to their goals in writing.[2]

Ten years later, the same individuals were found and surveyed once again. The 13 percent of individuals in the 1979 Harvard MBA Program who had set goals—even though not in writing—were earning on average twice as much as the 84 percent of their classmates who had not set goals. Sounds great to you? Keep reading to hear what is great:

The 3 percent of individuals who had clearly *written* goals ten years earlier were earning, on average, *ten times as much as the other 97 percent put together!*

The proof is in the pudding. Document your goals!

Action Step: Put your defined goals in writing.

Secret 7 for Creating Your Own Success: Take Control of Your Life

Let's face it: It takes a strong and confident person to stand up to the unpleasant situations that life deals you or that you unknowingly invited into your life.

It also takes a lot of willpower to face those unexpected challenges. A take-control approach is not for the weak of heart. Perhaps that is why it is one of the attributes of self-made millionaires and Secret 7.

Sarian Bouma, the fifth self-made millionaire interviewed for this book, definitely took control of her life. As shared in her biography, *Welfare to Millionaire: The Heart of a Winner*, she experienced the unexpected within five years after arriving in the United States from Sierra Leone, Africa. Her original intention for coming to "the land of the free" was to continue her education in communications after establishing a radio and television reputation for herself in her homeland during her teenage years.

During the first five years in the States, Sarian met who she thought was her Prince Charming, married, had a child, divorced, and found herself on welfare. The day that she had to feed her baby water because she did not have enough food stamps to buy milk was the day she took control of her life and turned it around.

Sarian began by taking responsibility and let go of the past. She met with a welfare counselor, who recommended that she apply to be in a bank training program through the center. She took the person's advice and was accepted.

After completing the training, she worked as a bank teller and, a few years later, as a credit union manager. She met her second husband, who noticed that she was bright, hard-working, and very personable in the workplace.

Sarian's spouse encouraged her to start a business doing something that she was good at. She gave a lot of thought to his advice and remembered receiving accolades from individuals whose private homes and commercial buildings she had cleaned during her first five years in the United States.

She began the process by applying for a small business loan and wrote on the application that someday the office of the President of the United States would be on her list of clients. Four years later, she earned the contract for the new Executive Office Building where the President's staff works.

Sarian Bouma founded Capitol Hill Building Maintenance Inc. in June 1987. Her award-winning, multi-million-dollar corporation employed more than 200 individuals.

Sarian became a self-made millionaire in her mid-thirties. She says that her strength lies in her tenacity.

Three Tips for Taking Control of Your Life

1. Identify your strengths and weaknesses. Focus on the strengths that you have and gradually transform your weaknesses into strengths.

2. Have a positive sense of self. Read books on enhancing your self-esteem and self-confidence. This way, when you find yourself at one of life's crossroads, you will act more decisively rather than second-guessing your decision.

3. Avoid "paralysis analysis" (overthinking situations). Instead, give yourself a deadline for taking control of unexpected situations. The worst decision is often no decision.

Action Step: Take control of your life by managing even the smallest details. This will prepare you for better handling the big challenges that come your way.

They Have a Strong Work Ethic

Secret 8 for Creating Your Own Success: Keep Your Word

Are you a promise-maker or a promise-breaker? People often measure your worth based on how well you keep your word. Being accountable for doing what you say you are going to do is an essential quality for becoming a self-made millionaire.

Did you know that making a commitment to keep your word begins with you first keeping your word to yourself? For instance, when you tell yourself that you are going to eliminate sugar from your diet, do you? When you say that you are going to get eight hours of sleep a night, do you? Or when you commit to yourself that you are going to begin exercising five times a week, do you? Keeping your word begins with keeping promises to yourself.

Successful people do what they say they are going to do. Commitments are often made with a mere exchange of words. A perfect example is the relationship that Mickey Redwine, founder of Dynamic Cable Holdings and the twenty-first self-made millionaire interviewed for this book, has had with one of his largest customers.

In one particular case, fiberoptic cables were cut leaving thousands of customers without service. Because time was of the essence to remedy the situation, there was not time for the company to bid out the project or to complete paperwork for Mickey's services. The relationship to do the work worth millions of dollars was based on mere trust.

Are you a person of your word or are you known as an individual whose actions do not match what you say? Oftentimes people use phrases such as "I'll call you later" or "I'll call tomorrow" as empty phrases. Those on the receiving end often take these words at face value and expect to receive a call by the times mentioned. When they do not, the person who mouthed the words loses credibility with the other person.

Recognize that your trustworthiness is on the line when you promise to do something by a given time and do not follow through.

Three Ways to Keep Your Word

1. When you say that you are going to do something, write it down. Your words then become real and you are more likely to follow through.

2. When you promise something by a given time, do it! You will establish credibility with the other person by keeping your word.

3. Avoid making excuses when you have been caught in the act of not doing what you said you were going to do. Rebuild credibility with both yourself and others by following through the next time you make a promise.

ACTION STEP: DEVELOP A STRONG SENSE OF CREDIBILITY WITH OTHERS BY DOING WHAT YOU SAY YOU ARE GOING TO DO.

Secret 9 for Creating Your Own Success: Be a Person of Integrity

Most of us do not stay up at night analyzing our morals. What I can tell you for certain is that you know you have integrity when it is put to the test.

Let me tell you about Connie L., the sixth self-made millionaire in this book, who reaped big dividends thanks to her integrity.

Connie describes herself as growing up very poor. When she started working, she felt that she was successful when she was able to pay a bill as soon as it came in rather than waiting for a paycheck.

After taking on the position as office manager/bookkeeper at a company, she could not figure out why the organization was unable to pay their bills when they were bringing in a lot of money.

Connie was asked by the president to research a former employee who he suspected was stealing from the company. In doing so, she noticed some things that didn't match. She soon discovered the reason for the company's financial issues started with the president and went all the way down to the crew, who were all taking their "piece of the pie."

Connie also discovered that there was an out-of-state owner who had no idea that the company had two sets of books. She started incorporating foolproof methods that made the team accountable for every ounce of material that went out the door, as well as requiring purchase orders for everything brought in. Numbers don't lie, and Connie was able to get the company back in the black once the thieving subdued. While doing this, she was compiling the data so the owner would have some ground to stand on. She spent the next eight months putting together the pieces and re-creating the entire company books for the previous five years and found more than $1,500,000 missing!

The toughest day of Connie's life was telling the out-of-state owner that his best friend, the one he set up in business, was the one stealing from him. The owner flew into town the next day and fired the president. He told Connie that if she helped him turn the company around, he would give it to her. Not thinking he was serious, Connie ran the company as if it were her own. She loved her job and had flexible hours.

Connie was shocked when the company owner called her in 2006 and said he was ready to make good on his promise and turn the company over to her. She wasn't sure what he meant when he signed off on the last document and stated, "One day you are going to be a very wealthy young lady." He wrote her a letter that shared how touched he was that a stranger came in and saved him.

Note: Besides being a person of integrity, Connie is incredibly unassuming. She did not know that she had achieved millionaire status until the producer for Blue Collar Millionaires contacted her. She said that she thought they were knocking on the wrong door. Only when she qualified for the taping did she realize that she was a millionaire. Talk about integrity paying off!

Four Ways to Display Your Integrity

1. Keep your word. When you say that you are going to have an answer for someone by a specific time, contact the person by the time promised—or earlier—whether you have the information or not.

2. Be honest. When you make a mistake, "own it" rather than placing blame. Losers point fingers.

3. Be ethical. When you know something is morally wrong, deal with it rather than looking the other way.

4. Be respectful. Be as thoughtful to security guards and custodians as you are to your manager.

ACTION STEP: RATE YOUR LEVEL OF INTEGRITY THE NEXT TIME IT IS PUT TO THE TEST.

Habit 5

They Set Priorities

Secret 10 for Creating Your Own Success: Be a Time Master

Successful people treat time as a valuable commodity. Self-made millionaires have a clear definition of what they want to accomplish before getting out of bed in the morning.

Some of the thirty individuals interviewed for this book are early birds and find that they can get a lot accomplished before the crack of dawn. Others are night owls and find that their most productive time of day is late at night until the wee hours of the morning. And others do both!

Here are a few of their comments:

"I believe in starting my day early and usually have accomplished more by 8:00 a.m. than most do in an entire day." —Connie L.

"I get up early and exercise, eat a healthy breakfast, and complete five hours of work before lunch."—Mike Vetter

"Don't waste a minute and don't waste a movement. I start early and end late." —Dru Riess

"Get up earlier than anyone else. Stay later than anyone else." —Bunny Lightsey

"Be prepared to put in thirty hours a day, because twenty-four hours is simply not enough." —Sarian Bouma

Six Strategies for Mastering Your Time

1. Plan your work and then work your plan. Create a road map about what you intend to accomplish each evening for the following twenty-four hours. This action will free up your mind.

2. Balance your list with both work and play. After creating your list, evaluate the purpose of each action item. Label them as "need to accomplish" and "would like to accomplish." For instance, your list may look like this:

   > **Need** to prospect for new business relationships.

   > **Need** to maintain an existing business relationship.

   > **Want** to spend dinner with family members.

   > **Want** to exercise.

   > **Want** to create time to think.

3. When something comes to mind that you need to do, schedule time to do it the following day. If it is a last-minute priority, reprioritize your "Would like to accomplish" with your "Need to accomplish" task.

4. Free up your mind. When something comes to mind that you need to do, write it down rather than storing it in your mind.

5. Touch mail once—or not at all. Time masters do their best to touch things once—or not at all—by automating bills. When receiving bills via snail mail, they open and pay them at once rather than setting them aside to pay later.

6. Monetize your minutes. Review your week's priorities. Assign a dollar value to your tasks. Recognize that spending time with family, exercising, and taking time to think are priceless!

ACTION STEP: TREAT EACH HOUR OF THE DAY WITH THE SAME RESPECT YOU WOULD TREAT A $1,000 BILL.

Secret 11 for Creating Your Own Success: Be Punctual

Show me a person who is late and I will show you someone who will never make it to self-made-millionaire status. Sound a little harsh? Perhaps it is. Sometimes, however, the truth hurts.

For the past fifteen years, I have been analyzing the relationships that people have with time. I am convinced that people who are early or punctual are more self-disciplined than those who run late.

People who can manage their time can also manage their money. Let me prove my theory to you. Write down the name of a person. Next to the individual's name, write down "E" if the person is typically *early*, "O" if the person is typically *on time*, or "L" if the person *runs consistently late.*

If the individual whose name you have written has an "L" next to it, I would venture to say that the person also has a poor mastery of his or her finances. If you say that is not the case then the person is probably a trust fund baby! If you wrote "E" or "O" next to the individual's name, I would venture to say that the person has a good mastery of their finances. Have I proven to you the "if you can manage your time, you can manage your money" theory?

George Schaefer, former CEO and chairman of the board of Fifth Third Bank had a punctuality mantra for his employees: "When you are five minutes early, you are ten minutes late." Having consulted with this bank client for more than twenty-five years, I can say that 99.9 percent of their team arrived at my programs either before the start of the meeting time or on time. It is all about setting the expectation.

So, if you are reading the section of this book and can relate to being early or on time, congratulations. You definitely have what it takes to be a self-made millionaire. On the other hand, if you are notoriously late, there is still hope if you are willing to put this secret into practice.

Here are two guidelines for becoming a punctuality convert:

1. **Write down the time you have to leave.** When you are scheduled to be somewhere by a specific time, write down the time that you have to leave rather than the time that you have to be there.

2. **Build in extra time to arrive at appointments.** This will minimize your stress level, especially when you are in that unexpected traffic jam.

The peripheral benefit of mastering this secret is that it will automatically carry over to the way you manage your finances. Just wait and see.

ACTION STEP: WHEN GOING TO A SCHEDULED MEETING, WRITE DOWN THE TIME YOU HAVE TO LEAVE RATHER THAN THE TIME YOU HAVE TO BE THERE.

Secret 12 for Creating Your Own Success: Stay Focused

The power of focus may sound like an easy secret to many; however it is a challenging one until mastered. Successful people recognize that concentrating on completing *one project at a time* is much less time consuming and certainly less labor intensive.

Erroneously, people who multi-task may "feel" more productive because they are doing several things at once. For instance, they may be working on a project, hear an email ding, read it and then respond to the email message, return to the project at hand, receive a text message ten minutes later, step away from the project to respond to the text, and then return to the project at hand once again. No wonder the project takes two to four times longer to complete! It also adds to work frustration.

Let me give you a recent example. During autumn 2017, I was presenting a training program for one of my energy company clients. When I asked the senior account managers in attendance what they found to be the most stressful part of their positions, several of them said that they spend more time "reacting" each day getting things crossed off on their daily list. They said that they felt pulled in different directions during the work day from assignments with deadlines to customers calling with complaints, to email messages from other departments, and the list went on.

A seasoned account manager in attendance stepped up to the plate to offer his colleagues a solution. He reminded them of the words from Charles Winchester (in the television series *M*A*S*H*). This sagely advice was: "Do one thing at a time. Do it well and then move on." Many of his colleagues acted as though they had an epiphany. They realized that they do not have to act like Pavlov's dog every time they receive an email message or telephone call. Rather than "reacting" to every ding, they recognized that their time could be used much more effectively by doing one thing at a time, doing it well, and *then* moving on.

Rather than letting distractions control you, do what successful people do who have mastered the power of focus. One way to do this is by taking a proactive approach by turning off anything that dings. Create an environment free from noise and people stimulation. Rather than being anti-social, actually schedule time and a location for yourself when and where you can best concentrate.

Also, schedule an appointment with yourself. List the date, beginning and end time, and location where you will meet yourself. Be specific about the project that requires your undivided attention. Let nothing get in the way of your "focus appointment." The more specific you are about what you want to accomplish, the more productive this scheduled time will be.

Because I am easily distracted, I schedule my "focus time" around 4:30 a.m. I get up and let out the dog as the coffee is brewing. I meet myself in my work area at 5:00 a.m. and work on the most challenging project that I have to accomplish that day until 7:30 a.m. It is truly amazing what can be accomplished in two and a half hours of uninterrupted time.

Kristen Souza, the seventh self-made millionaire in this book, confirmed how important the power of focus has been to her and her husband in achieving their seven-million-dollar net worth. Kristen says that the way she focuses is by not allowing distractions, interruptions, and time-wasting practices to deter her from what is most important. The success secrets certainly worked for them. These Hawaiian natives are globally recognized leaders in the handmade ukulele industry.

If "staying focused" is a success secret that you have yet to master, here are four steps to get you there:

1. Schedule an appointment with yourself. List the location, beginning and end time, and task at hand.

2. Create an agenda for yourself. List what you intend to accomplish and the steps you will take to meet this daily goal.

3. When starting the meeting with yourself, review your intended goal and then get started. If your mind wanders, simply refocus and continue to work.

4. As you near your meeting end time, schedule the next "focus meeting" with yourself.

Once you create a routine, you will appreciate these private meetings with yourself. You also will become more time efficient by mastering the power of focus.

ACTION STEP: EACH AND EVERY DAY, SCHEDULE A SPECIFIC BEGINNING AND END TIME, LOCATION, AND PROJECT ON WHICH TO FOCUS.

They Have a Thirst for Knowledge

Secret 13 for Creating Your Own Success: Be a Lifelong Learner

Think about it: You probably have spent the majority of the first eighteen to twenty-two years of your life learning. You learned to walk, talk, and become a social creature. You learned reading, writing, and arithmetic. You learned the field/trade of your choice for making a living and hopefully enjoy doing it most of the time. You stayed in that field or used it as a launching pad to find a field that you love.

After formal schooling ended, did your learning curve begin to flatten? Did you begin to engage in non-learning activities during your free time?

If you are like most, you spend your free time surfing the web. You spend hours on Facebook, or watch a Netflix movie or your favorite television program. Though that is fine, it is not a substitute for continuing to learn.

People who strive to be successful minimize their non-learning time. Instead they use their time productively to better themselves in order to ensure their learning curve continues its journey north. Hobbies are acquired, passions are discovered, reading books and hands-on exploration take place.

Lifelong learners continue to accumulate knowledge. Thomas C. Corley, who you met in Secret 5, spent five years researching habits of 177 self-made millionaires. In his 2016 book, *Change Your Habits, Change Your Life*, Corley shares that 87 percent of these individuals devote thirty minutes or more a day to reading. Rather than doing so for entertainment, he found they read books to both acquire and maintain knowledge. Corley found that self-made millionaires read three types of books: biographies, self-help or personal development, and history.[1]

Think about it: Reading thirty minutes a day would be equivalent to reading the equivalent of thirty books a year. (Note: The average adult reading speed is between two and three hundred words per minute.)

According to the Pew Research Internet's Group Poll, however, the average adult in the United States reads a mere five books a year.[2] Hmmm. A few books to go to catch up with these self-made millionaires.

Here are four ways to master becoming a lifelong learner without looking for more hours in the day:

1. Schedule a specific time each day for your lifelong learning journey. You are more likely to do it when it is preplanned.

2. Make what you may consider "down time" up time. If it is your learning style, listen to a podcast or audio book on the way to work. Prepare to use your time wisely as you

wait for that doctor who could use a time management course. You will begin using what used to be wasteful time as part of your thirty daily minutes of lifelong learning.

3. Choose to read, listen to, and experience from others based on what you strive to be. If you want to be great, read about accomplished people. If you want to overcome a challenge in your life, read about people who did just that.

4. Lifelong learning exercises your mind. Besides boosting brain power, you will be mastering one success secret.

ACTION STEP: SCHEDULE THIRTY MINUTES A DAY TO BEGIN YOUR LIFELONG LEARNING JOURNEY.

Secret 14 for Creating Your Own Success: Learn Something New Every Day

One way successful people get their creative juices flowing is by learning something new every day. Some gather new information related to their areas of expertise. Others take time to learn a new skill.

These go-getters schedule time on their calendars to challenge both their mind and body. It may be as simple as listening to a podcast, reading the morning paper, or taking a golf lesson.

Reading

Self-made millionaires read for different reasons than the average American. The average American reads for pleasure and also to de-stress whereas most self-made millionaires choose topics to make their heads and minds rich. Although some read mystery and other nonfiction books written by their favorite authors, the majority of them focus on three areas of interest: self-improvement, biographies, and history, as shared in Secret 13 (Be a Lifelong Learner). One reason for these types of books is to learn from others' experiences and find out how they handled similar situations that they may be encountering.

Doing

Whether it is a vigorous activity like tennis or one that is not a physical sport such as golf, both sports are top choices for self-made millionaires. Perhaps it is because they are social and challenging sports that require skill and concentration. These sports also are great ones for refining decision-making skills, another secret that is vital for creating your own success. Though business may not officially take place on the tennis court or golf course, ethics and interpersonal relations are important parts of these sports—two more secrets for creating your own success.

Listening

Successful people recognize that a wonderful way to learn is by listening to others. Whether they agree or not with the other person, they are learning a new perspective.

Three Ways to Learn Something New Every Day

1. Search for events in your local area. See which are of most interest to you. Then schedule time to attend one or more of them. You will be sure to learn something new that day.

2. Download or buy a hard copy of a book about someone who has succeeded in your field of interest. Learn from the success and failure of the person.

3. Listen more than you talk. As the saying goes, "You were given two ears and one mouth."

ACTION STEP: SCHEDULE AN ACTIVITY IN WHICH YOU HAVE NEVER PARTICIPATED.

Habit 7

They Stay Organized

Secret 15 for Creating Your Own Success: Become a Minimalist

Many people are rich based on their belongings. Does that describe you? If you had bought fewer "things," how could that have increased your net worth?

Studies have shown that people hold on to things for sentimental reasons or because they think they may need that item someday.

Teresa Bullock Cohen, a licensed independent clinical social worker, shares why people have such a hard time letting go of things: "People hold on to things based on a fear of deprivation."[1] She points out that it is easier for the brain not to make a decision, which is one reason that people do not let go of material things that are no longer of use to them.

Most self-made millionaires, however, do not hold on to things. Instead, a trait that they possess is minimalism. They keep their lives simple by following the "quality rather than quantity rule." They recognize that "less is more." That includes making fewer decisions about what to wear, what to buy, where to go, what to eat, and so forth. Fewer things mean fewer decisions.

Don't be fooled into believing that these successful people deprive themselves. On the contrary, minimalists conserve their energy for big decisions that impact their lives and others rather than wasting time on trivial things that will not matter in a week, a month, or a year. For instance, minimalists do not waste time figuring out what to wear. Mark Zuckerberg, Tim Cook, Warren Buffett, and Jeff Bezos wear the uniforms of their choice: a t-shirt and jeans, a suit, or a polo shirt and slacks. Fewer decisions create more room for a clear mind.

These individuals live with less in order to focus more on what they consider important: financial freedom, healthy relationships, family/friend time, and a business that they love.

You may be asking yourself, "Is it worth becoming a minimalist?" Absolutely—if you want to simplify your life.

Five Advantages of Becoming a Minimalist

1. You will feel more organized. You will be more orderly with fewer "things."

2. You will think more clearly. Fewer things, fewer distractions.

3. You will be more time efficient. You will be able to find things faster.

4. You will be more productive. Eliminating unnecessary "things" frees you up to focus on decisions that can make a difference in your life and that of others.

5. Your surroundings will feel larger with less clutter. What an easy way to acquire more square footage at no additional cost.

When you are ready to test what it feels like to become a minimalist, choose the one hundred things in your life that you consider essential. That includes what you wear, your accessories, your toiletries, your kitchen items, your technology tools, and so on. Keep everything else out of sight, whether that means covering the clothes that are not on your list with a sheet, boxing the toiletries that you will not be using, utilizing a special drawer in your bedroom and bathroom for your chosen toiletries, using only one cupboard in the kitchen, and so forth. (Note: Furniture, photos, cars, and bikes do not count as part of your one hundred items.)

Are you ready? Get set. Now list your one hundred items.

Use the items on your list exclusively for one month and see how your life is transformed. See how many fewer decisions you make regarding what to wear. Notice how much less time you are spending finding something now that you have less clutter surrounding you. You also will have less distractions and be able to think more clearly.

Three Steps to Becoming a Minimalist

1. Create a dress uniform. Most of us wear the same thing every day anyway. Whether it is a suit, jeans and a t-shirt, black slacks, or that little black dress, keep your choice of clothes from which you have to choose to a minimum. You can accentuate your outfits with the ten to twenty accessories that you may want to include in the one hundred items that you choose to keep in your life.

2. Make a list of what you use on a daily basis. Most of us are creatures of habit. Do you use the same mug, eat on your favorite plate, and use the same toiletries? By creating this list, you will narrow down what you use and minimize the clutter that surrounds your-soon-to-be one hundred most-used items.

3. Identify who you are rather than what you have. By following this guideline, you will see material things in a completely different light. In fact, you will place less emphasis on "things" and focus more on your quality of life and the people who you choose to be around.

ACTION STEP: LIVE WITH ONE HUNDRED ITEMS FOR THE NEXT MONTH. AFTER THAT, DECIDE WHAT YOU DID NOT MISS. THEN SELL THEM OR GIVE THEM AWAY.

Secret 16 for Creating Your Own Success: Plan Ahead

Many people live life by the seat of their pants. They react to what is happening on a day-to-day basis instead of mapping out each day, week, month, and year.

Successful people, on the other hand, protect their time. They plan both their work time and hours in their personal life. They map out their time with the same attention to detail that they preplan their purchases.

As you will see in many of the fifty two secrets in this book, planning is an essential part of the success of these self-made millionaires. They plan their time, they preplan their purchases, and they plan their financial road map. They are master planners.

You can call them control freaks; I call them masters of their own destiny.

People who plan ahead are more organized. They can handle the unexpected easier. This is due to the fact the majority of their life is planned out.

As shared in Secret 10, people who are good time masters also are in control of their finances. They plan ahead.

Why not test how good you are at planning ahead? Write down what you did for the past twenty-four hours. Now list next to your actions what percentage was planned versus spontaneous. How many of your actions were planned versus what others requested of you? If you found that more than 30 percent of your actions were based on other people's requests and doing things spontaneously, you may realize that you could do a better job of planning ahead.

Now, plan what you want tomorrow to look like. List what you want to accomplish both personally and professionally in one-hour increments. Be sure to build in relaxation time. Leave 20 percent of your time to be flexible.

Many people make planning ahead a New Year's resolution, but why wait? Make planning ahead a lifetime resolution beginning today.

Four Strategies for Planning Ahead

1. Plan your personal and professional life a month in advance. You will be surprised how freeing it is to be so organized. Leave 20 percent of your schedule open to allow for flexibility and other people's requests.

2. Recognize that you are creating your "tomorrow" by planning today.

3. Stay on task. By following your plan, you will be surprised how much more you will accomplish.

4. Build quiet time into your schedule.

ACTION STEP: PLAN YOUR WORK AND WORK YOUR PLAN.

Habit 8

They Are Efficient

Secret 17 for Creating Your Own Success: Build a Team

Eighty percent of the self-made millionaires interviewed for this book started their own businesses. These individuals would be the first to tell you that an essential secret for creating their own success was to identify individuals who had the necessary emotional intelligence and professional skills to be part of their team. They would also be the first to tell you that just as important as identifying qualified individuals is retaining them.

Brian Wong, the eighth self-made millionaire interviewed for this book, is a master at building a team. He focuses working *on* business as his team members work *in* business. This allows him to expend his energy to grow his mobile advertising company, Kiip. It must be an effective skill considering that Brian achieved self-made millionaire status at age twenty-one.

Jason Phillips, who you will read about in Secret 30, retains employees of Phillips Home Improvements by developing them into leaders. Jason emphasizes that you need a team who will stick together through thick and thin times. He recommends that you get the right people on your team through the use of behavior profiling, such as DISC. Recognize that everyone is not built like you are. You need to lead a team of diverse skills, personalities, and behavioral preferences.

Jason also has found documenting a system is essential for team members to clearly understand how to do their jobs. He recommends a system that is easy to understand, teach, and replicate. Good systems help people achieve great things.

Besides grooming their employees to be effective, they made a point of effectively managing and motivating them—two essential attributes for building an effective team. As good managers do, both Brian and Jason maintain clear communication with their teams by being accessible for them. In addition, they recognize the value of behavior modification by catching them "doing it right" when they are seen or heard handling customer complaints effectively or go over and above to complete a job in a timely manner.

Self-made millionaires set clear expectations through their own actions as well as through documented systems. These self-made millionaires have built outstanding teams by only expecting them to do what they have been seen doing themselves at one point.

These successful people also can attest to the fact that their teams treat customers and clients only as well as they are treated. They have learned that building an effective team means taking time to listen to them so that they in turn can lend an ear to customers and clients.

Four Ways to Build a Great Team

1. Recognize that the sum is greater than the whole. That includes knowing that an organization is only as good as each team member.

2. Keep your lines of communication open. Let team members know from the start that they have access to you. When there is something that can be done better, communicate it tactfully as a "teachable moment."

3. Catch them "doing it right." Your team members will enjoy working with you when they are acknowledged. A compliment goes a long way.

4. Differentiate *on business* versus *in business* roles. Remind your organization's rainmakers that they should spend the majority of their day working on business rather than working in business. Those in-business tasks should be delegated to their teams who have in-business responsibilities.

ACTION STEP: INVEST IN YOUR TEAM BY DEVELOPING THEM AS LEADERS. TRAIN AND EMPOWER THEM. YOUR BUSINESS WILL FLOURISH.

Secret 18 for Creating Your Own Success: Delegate

Are you a micromanager or a delegator? Successful people recognize that they create more time in the day for themselves through their art of delegating. Besides freeing up time to grow their business, they are developing their team by giving them more responsibility.

I could have earned an award for being the official micromanager—until I had the assignment of going around the world to train the private bankers of American Express Bank. Talk about a whirlwind tour! Between being in different time zones and full days of training, I had little communication with my assistant, who had been with me for ten years and knew my business inside and out.

When I returned to work three weeks later, I asked her for a business update. She proudly said that she "closed" three pieces of business. I was stunned and asked, "How?" Her response: "You left me alone!"

I was so proud of her and so embarrassed that I had undermined her abilities to have more responsibility than doing mere administrative work. My micromanaging skills quickly ended. From that day forward, my mighty assistant has had the responsibility of following up with potential clients and learning what we can do to earn their business.

I learned to become a master delegator by default. And so can you!

Delegation is an ongoing challenge for many leaders. Eli Broad echoes that. This American builder of two Fortune 500 companies says this about delegation: "The inability to delegate is one of the biggest problems I see with managers at all levels."[1]

Laura K., the ninth self-made millionaire interviewed for this book, became a top-producing loan officer for one of the nation's largest mortgage companies. Her secret: She learned to delegate to her two competent assistants. Delegation was a skill, however, that Laura learned only after she realized her career was consuming her life seven days a week. She described her life as being imbalanced.

Laura explained that she woke up one day and realized she only had two hands. Her business was booming and her planner was exploding with mortgage appointments. She could not figure out how she was going to maintain her existing client relationships and still find time to tackle the business opportunities that she had worked so hard to obtain.

Laura shared how this business dream dilemma taught her the power of delegation. Although she did not want to give up control of all of the details, she realized that if she was to get to the next income level (especially because she was working on straight commission), she had to redesign her business plan.

The first step began with trusting her assistants enough to delegate assignments to them. They became the backbone of her success as they handled the "back of the house" business such as loan processing. Laura found that the art of delegation not only empowered her team, it also freed up her time as the frontline person to both court and close more business. This gave her more energy and enthusiasm in every aspect of her life.

The more Laura delegated, the more she made a point of acknowledging her team members with both compliments for managing their workload and financial incentives. Her success became their success. Everyone won thanks to the power of delegating.

Laura made her first million in her mid-forties.

Four Tips for Mastering the Art of Delegation

1. Recognize that anything you have done three times should be delegated. Instead of organizing a meeting, delegate it. Rather that creating the meeting agenda, empower a team member to organize it.

2. Reward your team members with praise for the projects they have assumed. A kind word and display of appreciation will encourage them to want more responsibility.

3. When you see a mistake that a team member has made with a project that you have delegated, have that person "own" the error. Whatever you do, avoid taking back the project and doing it yourself. To err is human—once in a while.

4. After mastering the art of delegation, be sure to use your extra time wisely.

ACTION STEP: WRITE DOWN EVERYTHING YOU HAVE DONE AT WORK DURING THE PAST TWO DAYS. FIGURE OUT WHAT YOU COULD EASILY HAVE DELEGATED TO A TEAM MEMBER (ASSUMING YOU HAVE SOMEONE TO WHOM YOU CAN DELEGATE).

They Go That Extra Mile

Secret 19 for Creating Your Own Success: Take Calculated Risks

As I was writing several sections of this book in a coffee shop, brief conversations took place with the persons sitting within an arm's-length distance of me. One of these conversations was with an individual named Abed Elsamna, whom, within a few minutes of our conversation, I earmarked as a budding self-made millionaire. He had found his passion. He was innovative, he was a people person, and he asked until he got a "yes" (he had spent several months convincing his spouse, who was also in finance, that it would be worth the risk to leave his secure job in finance). Above all, he was willing to risk failure in order to experience success. Although I hardly knew him, I immediately noticed this twenty-nine-year-old had already mastered several of the fifty-two secrets for creating his own success.

For the past year, he and his cofounder, Hassan Mahmoud, had spent all of their free time at night, early mornings, and weekends developing a product for event venues. Their technology offered a new way for these small businesses to offer a modern, tech-enabled experience to their clients as they start planning their weddings or other events. After testing their product, Abed and Hassan were ready to dedicate 110 percent of their time to launching their new enterprise called Invitext Technologies.

This scenario is a common beginning path for many self-made millionaires. They start their careers as employees of an established organization. If the entrepreneurial bug strikes them or they find themselves unemployed, they take the leap. They begin their own businesses.

They do not allow the Small Business Administration (SBA) statistic that only 66 percent of small business will survive their first two years to discourage them.[1] In fact, they like being challenged (Secret 32).

This is a common beginning for many self-made millionaires. At least it was for Jeb Lopez, the tenth self-made millionaire in this book. Jeb was born in the Philippines and always dreamed of living in America. Jeb's dad offered to pay for college if he got accepted to school in the United States. Jeb got accepted and moved to California for college. After graduation, he landed a good IT job in Washington, DC. He soon realized, however, that the white-collar world was not for him.

Jeb quit his job and started volunteering for a non-profit organization. (Look what volunteering did for Jeb when he "gave back" in Secret 43). As a way of earning additional money, he took a temporary job delivering auto parts for a local auto dealership. He recognized there was a big opportunity to improve upon auto parts delivery services.

In 2011, with only $7,000, Jeb launched Wheelz Up, LLC, a business that delivers auto parts to dealers and body and repair shops in Washington, DC, Virginia, Maryland, and Texas. Six years later, his company generates more than $4.5 million annually.

Whereas 16 percent of the individuals randomly selected for this book achieved self-made millionaire status as employees in corporate America and one person invested in an already established business, the remaining 74 percent of individuals chose to either grow their own businesses or acquire existing ones.

How well do you handle taking risks? Do you envision your future as staying in a role with an established organization? Or do you have the entrepreneurial bug just waiting to come out?

Three Ways to Take Calculated Risks

1. Stretch yourself by taking small risks. You will build your confidence for larger risks and/or the unexpected unknowns that come your way.

2. As you prepare to take a risk, plan ahead. Ask yourself the best thing that would happen as well as the worst-case scenario. Create proposed solutions for both scenarios. Your risk tolerance will be improved when you prepare for the unknown.

3. Recognize that in order to succeed in life, you have to risk failure to experience success.

ACTION STEP: PREPARE YOURSELF FOR UPCOMING CALCULATED RISKS BY STRETCHING YOURSELF TO DO THINGS THAT ARE OUT OF YOUR COMFORT ZONE.

Secret 20 for Creating Your Own Success: Turn Failures Into Opportunities

Do you learn from past failures or make the same mistake multiple times?

Most of us instinctively learn from failure. It starts when we go from crawling to taking that first step. It is rare that our first step is the beginning of walking. What is more common is wobbling, stumbling, and even falling . . . and then starting again.

Based on the encouragement we receive from family and friends—as well as their inner strength—our confidence to turn failure into opportunities either increases or diminishes. Our inner core, that belief that we have in ourselves, sets the stage for how we handle what many people call "failures."

According to Thomas C. Corley, 27 percent of self-made millionaires have tried and failed at least once in business.[2] Factretriever.com states that the average millionaire goes bankrupt at least 3.5 times.[3]

Many people consider a failure in a negative light. They see something not working the way they intended it as a losing proposition, a dead end. They give up on their idea—perhaps too quickly.

Do you see failures as setbacks or as "a success in progress"? As you read in the first secret of this book, having a "millionaire mindset" is essential for creating your own success. I remember the impact that reading behavioral psychologist Dr. Eden Ryl's words had on me when I was in my early thirties. She said, "You have to risk failure to experience success. . . ."[3]

Have you ever failed? If you say no, I am not impressed. My question is: What is it that you are not doing to get out of your comfort cocoon? If you tell me that you have been offered every job for which you have applied, you are either fibbing or you have not applied for enough jobs that could allow you to develop your potential to its fullest.

If, on the other hand, you admit that you have experienced failure, my hat goes off to you for taking a risk. My next question to you is "How did you turn your failure into an opportunity?

If you give me 101 excuses why you gave up after failing by pointing your finger at others, a situation, or the economy, shame on you! Remember, losers make excuses. Winners, on the other hand, find solutions by learning from the past and marching forward. Here are two common situations that describe people staying in their comfort zones rather than risking failure to potentially experience success:

1. Individuals are miserable in their current jobs, yet stay in them for fear of not finding another one. They do not want to risk failure by not finding a job that may be better suited for them.

2. People often stay in unhealthy relationships rather than learning how to make better the relationships they have. They do not realize that a healthy relationship is not about the other person's habits changing. It begins with how they react to the other person's habits.

Five Steps for Turning a Perceived Failure Into an Opportunity

1. Analyze what you could have done differently.

2. Figure out how you can modify your approach.

3. Be open to advice from others, specifically individuals who have accomplished similar goals. Get their perspectives about what they see you could have done differently.

4. Take the "As God is my witness, I will do it" Scarlet O'Hara approach. Allow failures to make your conviction to accomplish your goal even stronger. Then pick yourself up, brush yourself off, and try, try again.

5. Remember: You only have to be right once to succeed!

As Andy Hidalgo, one of the self-made millionaires in this book says, "If you try and fail, at least you learn but if you fail to try, you will never know how good you can become. Don't let failure stop your ambition. Stay positive and always look for opportunities. Be resourceful."

ACTION STEP: THE NEXT TIME THAT YOU FAIL, SEE IT AS "SUCCESS IN PROGRESS!"

Secret 21 for Creating Your Own Success: Persevere

Oftentimes when you read about successful people, what is not revealed are the perceived obstacles that they encountered along the way. What differentiates these individuals from others is how they manage "the unexpected." Rather than feeling defeated by unforeseen circumstances that the average Joe may perceive as "failure," these successful individuals have developed a "success mentality." They see a setback as an obstacle to be overcome. In other words, they persevere.

Successful individuals do not entertain the thought of giving up. The term *failure* is not in their vocabulary. Instead, successful people use their time and energy to figure out what it will take to get back on track and ultimately get the job done.

Mike Vetter, the twelfth self-made millionaire interviewed for this book, certainly has "perseverance" as part of his DNA.

As the owner and operator of The Car Factory, headquartered in Daytona Beach, Florida, Mike builds and sells one-of-a-kind unique concept cars for a living. Mike explained what sets him apart from 90 percent of the people who set out to build their own exotic cars is his positive mindset and perseverance. Though others may have extensive mechanical and automotive knowledge, many do not have the mental tenacity to keep going when they encounter an unforeseen obstacle.

When asked how he perseveres through setbacks, he shared his success belief by explaining: "My mindset is that there is no job that cannot be completed. When this mindset block occurs—*and it always does*—you must go on. When I encounter roadblocks, I break them down into smaller steps."

Mike has found that when he is challenged by an unforeseen obstacle, he works through the challenge and then sets a new goal regarding how he is going to achieve what needs to be redone. Mike shared that oftentimes, though he cannot always see the entire path of a project, the path does appear as he works toward his goal.

Four Steps to Persevere When You Encounter a Roadblock in Your Life

1. When you encounter an obstacle, write down how it occurred. By doing so, you will have a better chance of avoiding it in the future.

2. Write down possible solutions. Then one by one, prioritize which one will work the best for your present challenge.

3. Use the internet as a resource to learn how others have resolved similar challenges. You can be certain that you are not the first!

4. Above all, maintain a positive mindset. This attitude will give you the stamina to PERSEVERE.

ACTION STEP: THE NEXT TIME THAT YOU ENCOUNTER AN UNEXPECTED OBSTACLE IN YOUR LIFE, PERSEVERE!

Habit 10

They Develop a High
Emotional Quotient

Secret 22 for Creating Your Own Success:
Listen Up

You've learned how to read, but have you ever formally learned how to listen? If you have taken a class in effective listening and are putting the strategies into practice, my hat goes off to you. You are the exception.

Most people do not know how to listen—because they have never been taught. Perhaps that is why Listen Up is Secret 22 for Creating Your Own Success.

Listening is harder than it sounds. This skill is the differentiating factor between a businessperson with two ears and a business professional who gives his full attention when people are talking.

Having a high IQ does not qualify you as a good listener. Rather, individuals who have worked on developing a high EQ (emotional quotient) are better contenders for being good listeners than those with a mere high IQ.

So why is it that concentration while listening is a greater problem than concentration during any other form of communication? Ralph G. Nichols and Leonard A. Stevens, in their 1957 (yes, 1957) article, "Listening to People," explains why so many people are listening challenged:

> [W]e think faster than we talk. The average rate of speech for most Americans is 125 words per minute. Words race through our brains at speeds higher than 125 words per minute. . . . When we listen we ask our brains to receive words at an extremely slow pace compared to its capabilities.[1]

Though the way we communicate has changed dramatically since 1957, the art of listening has not improved. In fact, with the number of distractions that we have at our fingertips, the art of listening is on the decline.

Four Listening Tips

1. Stay in the moment. Give your *full* attention by eliminating distractions that could keep you from giving your 100 percent attention to the person(s) who is talking. That includes any form of technology that has the potential of beeping.

2. Let your body language and expressions demonstrate that you are listening. That means maintaining eye contact with the person talking, facing the person, avoiding crossed arms, nodding when you agree, and so forth.

3. Wait to be asked for your advice. Most people who need an ear simply want to be heard. Avoid giving unsolicited advice. Instead, only offer a solution when asked.

4. Echo what you heard the other person say. Summarize what you heard the other person say. Then offer your

solicited advice. This will both reinforce and clarify what you heard.

When you—and I—master *this* skill, I am confident that we will see each other at the end of the self-made millionaire finish line. Ready, set, listen!

ACTION STEP: ECHO WHAT YOU HEAR ANOTHER PERSON SAYING BEFORE GIVING ADVICE.

Secret 23 for Creating Your Own Success: Don't Be Afraid to Ask

Whether it was asking a question about something you do not understand or asking for a favor, successful people do not give it a second thought. They just ask!

I remember reading one of my favorite books, *The Instant Millionaire* by Mark Fisher. It was twenty-five years ago and I have read it fifty times (no kidding) since then.

One of the many lessons I learned from this book was *to not to be afraid to ask.* Let me give you a specific example when not being afraid to ask definitely helped.

After graduating from Ohio State University (Michigan fans: Please do not stop reading the book, but . . . Go Bucks!), I sent my resume to six high schools that had openings to teach Spanish the following school year. One week after the resumes were sent, I contacted each school district's superintendent's office to schedule face-to-face interviews.

I distinctly remember calling one superintendent's office only to learn from the administrative assistant that my resume had not been received. Because it was my first choice of districts where I wanted to be offered a job, I asked this administrative assistant who worked directly with the assistant superintendent if I could resend my resume once again and this time send it specifically to her attention. She agreed and I did just that.

Four days later, I called the school district's superintendent office. I reached my "new best friend" (at least in my mind) to confirm that she received my resume. She shared that she had indeed received my resume but that it might not be necessary to schedule an interview. The reason: At that very moment, the assistant superintendent was having a second interview with a job candidate for the Spanish teaching position for which I was interested.

At that point, I knew that I had nothing to lose and asked, "I moved to Cincinnati only one week ago and have selected your school district as my first choice for employment. May I ask you to be so kind as to slip a note under the door where this interview is taking place to request that the job candidate *not* be offered the position until after the assistant superintendent and I meet? I would be eternally grateful if you would help me."

Those five seconds of silence between the time I stopped talking and when I heard the administrative assistant respond seemed like an eternity. After sighing, she said that she would accommodate my request. Whew! I thanked her profusely and asked if I could call back the following day to see if the assistant superintendent would meet with me.

Two hours later the phone rang. It was the administrative assistant. She told me to be in their school district's office the following morning at 8:00 a.m. sharp.

Armed with a box of Godiva chocolates for my new best friend, I showed up at 7:45 a.m. the following day. And yes, after meeting with the assistant superintendent, learning about the position, then explaining why I wanted to be part of their school district, I was offered the job. I remained there for the first six years of my career. It definitely pays to ask!

Three Tips to Muster Up the Courage to Ask for Help

1. Put yourself in the place of the person who you are asking for help. If you would not think twice about helping someone who made the same request, then what are you waiting for? Ask!

2. Pay it forward. Do unsolicited favors for others and expect nothing in return. People benefitting from your generosity will appreciate it. They will also be more willing to help you when you reach out to them for help.

3. Make sure that you have more "you owe me" in the universe than "I owe you" favors in return. Your generosity to help others will give you the confidence to ask for help when you need it.

ACTION STEP: FOLLOW THE 21ST-CENTURY PLATINUM RULE OF "DOING ONTO OTHERS AS THEY WOULD WANT YOU TO DO UNTO THEM." BY DOING SO, WHEN YOU NEED A FAVOR, YOUR REQUEST WILL BE BETTER RECEIVED.

Secret 24 for Creating Your Own Success: Pay It Forward

A few years ago, I was walking down the street in Midtown New York. I glanced down only to see a wad of money on the ground. Apparently, it had fallen out of someone's pocket.

I picked it up and looked around to see if nearby pedestrians were retracing their footsteps to look for the treasure in my hand. There was no one in sight who fit that description. Without thinking twice, I stopped the next passerby and said, "Excuse me. Do you believe in paying it forward?" The person responded, "I sure do." I handed the wad of money to him and explained that I had found it on the ground a few minutes before and wanted to pay it forward. To this day, I do not know if the money amounted to $10 or $10,000. What I do know is that it wasn't mine to begin with and paying it forward was the right thing to do.

Most people know the dictionary term *pay it forward* as an expression describing the repayment of a good deed to someone other than the original giver, but few may know how it originated. Robert A. Heinlein's 1951 book *Between Planets* was made into a movie called *Pay it Forward* in 2000. The movie was about a boy who had a homework assignment about how to make a difference in the world. The student created the "pay it forward" theory, which was meant to create a ripple effect of good deeds throughout the globe.

The "pay it forward" principle has been and will continue to be a secret for creating your own success. This selfless act is a common trait in the life of the self-made millionaires interviewed for this book. They shared that they "paid it forward" by not only giving money to others, but also paying it forward by giving their time. The consensus for what they got back in return was unanimous: Doing good to others was in itself its own reward.

In fact, Jason Phillips, the eleventh self-made millionaire interviewed for this book, achieved this success status in his thirties. This most wholesome individual is the owner of Phillips Home Improvement based in Plano, Texas. He has seen the benefits of paying it forward. He shared that the peripheral benefits are "when he and his family enrich another life, our own is made richer."

When asked how Jason and his family paid it forward, here are a few of his selfless acts of both time and money:

> "One year, I saw the need to mentor children, many who lacked father figures. I did this by taking a day off work each week and teaching them martial arts and helping to build their character. I never saw the outcome and that was okay. I simply poured into their lives in faith as so many have poured into mine. As a byproduct, I was encouraged, and although I only worked a four-day week that year, God blessed our business with exponential growth."

> "We stopped and helped a stranger on the side of the road."

> "A man in front of us at the grocery store had a cart filled with baby food and diapers. When he checked out, his debit card did not work. My family and I had the opportunity to pay his bill."

> "We were prompted to give a Christmas present to a lady at a drive-thru window at a fast-food restaurant we frequented and it made her day."

As you see, you can pay it forward by giving to others in many ways. It can be as small a deed as a smile. It can be giving another person the parking space that you both spotted at the same time or paying for a stranger's meal for the sake of it. It may even be paying for a student's education without expecting anything in return. The size of the gesture is irrelevant. What is important is to do it without expecting anything in return.

Jason strongly believes in diligently sowing good seeds consistently. He shares that his success has been based on the "you reap what you sow" mentality. He says that paying it forward means doing the right thing when no one else is looking.

When was the last time you "paid it forward?" Following are a few ways you can make the world a better place.

Three Simple Ways to Pay it Forward

1. When you are driving in a lot of traffic, let the car at your side get in front of you.

2. Compliment a colleague for a job well done without expecting anything in return.

3. When you have been upgraded to first class on a flight, let the gate agent know that you would like to give your seat to another passenger sitting in coach without disclosing who did it. Now that's paying it forward!

ACTION STEP: THE NEXT TIME YOU HAVE AN OPPORTUNITY, PAY IT FORWARD! BESIDES MAKING SOMEONE ELSE'S DAY, YOU WILL EXPERIENCE A FEELING OF "NACHAS"—HEARTFELT HAPPINESS, AS THEY SAY IN YIDDISH.

Habit 11

They Nurture Their Bodies and Their Minds

Secret 25 for Creating Your Own Success: Exercise for the Health of It

According to the Center for Disease Control, only 20 percent of American adults are meeting the overall physical activity recommendations. Fifty percent are meeting the aerobic guidelines and a third are meeting the muscle-training recommendations.[1] People who seek a healthy, happy, and productive life, however, make physical exercise a regular part of their weekly activity. Successful people make a point of exercising regularly.

If you don't like exercising, think again. I admit that, like two-thirds of Americans, until starting to write this book, I did not have a regular exercise regime. My motivation for now exercising thirty minutes a day five times a week was learning that there is a direct correlation between physical fitness and brainpower. John J. Ratey, Harvard Medical School psychiatrist and author of *Spark: The Revolutionary New Science of Exercise and the Brain*, has found that even ten minutes of activity changes your brain.[2]

Besides being the thirteenth self-made millionaire in this book, Rodger DeRose, president and CEO of the Kessler Foundation, explained to me the lifelong benefits that he has personally found physical activity to have in both his personal and professional life. In fact, physical activity is second nature to Rodger.

He began when he was in grade school by participating in football, basketball, track, and baseball. In high school, he was active in the same team sports.

By the time he got to college, however, between working part time and taking full-time classes, Rodger could not find the time to participate in team sports. Rather than eliminating physical fitness from his life, he made a point of exercising daily.

Rodger's experience confirms Dr. Ratey's findings. He found that the benefits of exercise were far more than just keeping fit and trim. Rodger found that exercise benefited his sleep quality and energy level. It also helped him to manage stress and kept his mind clear—allowing him to compartmentalize activities better for the day ahead. Rodger even found that sixty to ninety minutes in the gym continues to help him set and achieve goals as well as manage his time more effectively.

Rodger was right when he explained that most successful people push themselves physically and mentally, which is why many of them have exercise routines that push their boundaries. It makes them physically stronger while improving their mental alertness. He is living proof to show that there is evidence that exercise is the single best investment a person can make for their brain in terms of mood, memory, and learning.

Three Ways to Make an Exercise Regime Part of Your Life

1. Commit to a specific time each day to exercise a minimum of thirty minutes.

2. If you will be working out offsite, pack your workout clothes in your gym bag the night before. If you have a gym in the building where you live, dedicate a specific drawer or section in your closet for your workout clothes.

3. Whether your exercise regime consists of jogging, swimming, joining a gym, or exercising in your own home, just do it! I can tell you first hand that you will be reenergized both mentally and physically!

ACTION STEP: MAKE EXERCISE PART OF YOUR WEEKLY ROUTINE.

Secret 26 for Creating Your Own Success: Take Time to Think

How many hours a week do you schedule time to think? I mean, really step aside from the everyday hubbub of life and actually *think?*

The first time I met someone who "scheduled" time to think was in 1992: John Pierce, an investment counselor who my accountant recommended I meet. (Little did he or I know that twenty-six years later, he would be the fourteenth self-made interviewed for in this book.) Before talking business, I asked John about one habit he had that attributed to his success. His response has stayed with me for more than twenty-five years:

"I find ways to unplug and actually think. I do silent weekend retreats that force contemplation."

John's response was the last answer I would have expected from this Type A macho guy who was climbing the slippery ladder of success. He actually took time to step away from his fast-paced life in order to "take time to think"?

As I was driving home alone from work that evening, John's words came back to me. Although I had never formally taken time to think, I realized that I had indeed experienced what he meant a few times in my life.

It had been when I was in the shower. I thought that the "aha" moment, that answer to the solution I had been pondering came by mere happenstance. Not at all. It had been because I had been alone, in a calm, unrushed environment, without distractions. Without realizing it, besides cleansing my body, I had unknowingly created an environment to also cleanse my mind and had made room "to think."

You are never too young or too old to take time to think. In Bill Gates, Sr.'s book, *Showing Up for Life,* he describes an instance when he caught his nine-year-old son, Bill Gates III, taking time to think. Bill Gates III's parents and siblings were in the car waiting for him to come out of the house. When he finally showed up, his Mom asked, "Bill, where were you?" He answered, "I was thinking, Mom. Don't you guys ever think?"[3]

Scheduling time to think must work. It did for Bill Gates III, a billionaire many times over. It did for John Pierce, who is now a self-made millionaire.

It can for you. Schedule time in your life "to think."

Three Benefits of Taking Time to Think

1. You will recharge your brain making the challenges of the day easier to handle.

2. That solution to the situation you have been working on resolving may come to you.

3. You may be a better listener after taking time to hear yourself think.

ACTION STEP: MAKE A DAILY APPOINTMENT WITH YOURSELF TO THINK. IF YOU ARE A MULTI-TASKER LIKE ME, TAKE FIVE EXTRA MINUTES IN THE SHOWER.

Habit 12

They Associate With Like-Minded People

Secret 27 for Creating Your Own Success: Surround Yourself With People You Want to Be Like

We all make choices that have a major impact on our lives. One of them is selecting with whom we choose to spend the most time.

Most people select their company randomly based on the people with whom they work, common interests, and family ties. Successful people in-the-making, however, have different criteria. They make a point of surrounding themselves with people they aspire to be like.

Robert Kiyosaki, author of the *Rich Dad Poor Dad* book series says, "The four people with whom you spend the most time is who you become in the future."[1] His words definitely hold true. Think about it. You are the product of both your environment and the people with whom you spend the most time. The actions, beliefs, and mindset of those individuals influence both your aspirations and who you become tomorrow both personally and professionally.

As they were reaching for success, self-made millionaires consciously selected individuals whom they identified as positive influencers. When they had access to these people, they asked them to mentor them. When they did not have access to these "people of influence," rather than lowering their bar and choosing "within reach" influencers, they read about the people who they aspired to be like, individuals who had the belief, the confidence, and the know-how to achieve.

Bruce Schindler, the fifteenth self-made another millionaire interviewed for this book, is living proof that surrounding yourself with individuals you want to be like works. Although he grew up in an impoverished environment, at an early age Bruce became keenly aware that people outside his home environment lived happy, healthy lifestyles that did not consist of addiction, abuse, and food stamps.

When spending time with his friends' families, this other way of life taught him to forge ahead by getting out of literal and emotional poverty. Like many, Bruce knew that he wanted to achieve a better life, yet had no idea about how to get there.

Bruce shared that his junior high school teacher was his first influencer. He once advised him with the following words: "You can choose your friends, so choose carefully. Surround yourself with the people you admire." Although most people were out of Bruce's family's socioeconomic league, he made a point of associating with individuals who lived a better life than he knew. As a result, these people inspired Bruce by giving him a sense of direction. Exposure to their lives and values also helped Bruce to clarify the life that he wanted.

After graduating from college, Bruce moved to Skagway, Alaska, in 1993. Bruce found his passion chasing mammoths (chasingmammoths.com). He founded Schindler Carvings and is responsible for carving and restoring fossilized ivory that has been buried under the ground for more than 35,000 years. Bruce became a self-made millionaire at thirty-five and is now an influencer for others.

Four Ways to Surround Yourself With People You Want to Be Like

1. Create a success road map for yourself. Write down the steps it will take in order to achieve *your success.*

2. Research individuals who have accomplished similar goals. Look for them by doing an online search. Also, look to your immediate left and right. They may be closer to you than you think.

3. When you gain access to these individuals either in person or by reading about their lives, document what it took for them to achieve their success. Then integrate those skills into your success journey.

4. Be sure to put Secret 24 (Pay It Forward) into practice. Individuals of influence will "show up" in your life as a result of the law of circulation.

ACTION STEP: REEVALUATE THE PEOPLE WITH WHOM YOU SPEND THE MOST TIME.

Secret 28 for Creating Your Own Success: Find a Brain Trust Advisor

When I was in my thirties, I was introduced to Napoleon Hill's book *Think and Grow Rich*. As I read it, I came across a term that I found fascinating: *brain trust advisors*. This term has remained in the forefront of my mind for the past several decades as I hired advisors for my consulting business.

When interviewing the thirty self-made millionaires for this book, the term *brain trust* was mentioned by several of these individuals. This is how "Find a Brain Trust Advisor" was selected to be Secret 28 for Creating Your Own Success.

You may be wondering how this term was created in the first place. James Kieran, a *New York Times* reporter, coined *brain trust* to describe the group of intellectual advisors who Franklin D. Roosevelt selected to help him during his 1932 presidential campaign.[2]

A brain trust refers to a group of individuals who are asked to provide counsel for achieving a specific goal or giving advice for solving challenging situations. Franklin D. Roosevelt apparently chose well. With advice from his "brain trust" advisory group, he was elected the thirty-second president of the United States. President Roosevelt also kept "Brain Trust Groups" to help him form the New Deal between 1933 and 1936.

If you are an employee at an organization, you may have been assigned a mentor. If you have not, take the initiative by asking an accomplished individual who is at least one professional level above you to be your mentor.

If you are an existing small business owner or intend to begin an enterprise, carefully select one or more brain trust advisors based on your short-term and long-term organization goals.

Select an individual who has mastered similar goals even if the person represents a complete different industry.

Chuck Ceccarelli, the sixteenth self-made millionaire interviewed for this book, inventor of the SidePuller™ and owner of In The Ditch Towing, says, "There's never been a successful company or person who did not have a brain trust group consisting of one of more individuals for advice and counsel."

Brain trust advisors come in many forms. An example of commonly used professional counsel/brain trust advisors are accountants, attorneys, pension administrators, and individuals on boards of directors. Personal brain trust advisors are often family members, friends, and other individuals who are casually or formally asked for their opinions based their past professional experience. In either case, these brain trust advisors offer objective advice based on what they have seen successfully work. Self-made millionaires in the making take the advice of these brain trust advisors and then use it (or not) as they see fit.

Recognize that your brain trust advisors may rotate based on changing needs. Some of these advisors remain in place. For example:

> ➤ Allan S., the first self-made millionaire in this book, described in Secret 3 (Find Your Passion), had more than thirteen brain trust advisors throughout his career. They consisted of his teachers who taught, advised, and counseled him to become an accomplished professional violinist. His advisors changed based on the musical ability that he developed over a sixteen-year period.

> ➤ Bruce Schindler, who you read about in Secret 27 (Surround Yourself With People You Want to Be Like), found his junior high school teacher as his brain trust

advisor. Thirty years later, in addition to becoming his trusted friend, this individual remains an important part of Bruce's personal advisory group.

Your selection of brain trust advisors or mentors should be based on what you want to achieve. It is important to revisit your selection of a brain trust advisor(s) and either replace or add "counsel" based on your changing needs and the needed expertise from these individuals.

Let me give you a specific situation when I needed to change brain trust advisors. In 1992, five years after beginning my U.S.-based consulting business, our firm received a request from two individuals in Taiwan. They wanted to buy a business license to duplicate for Taiwanese professionals what our firm was providing to individuals in the U.S. professional services sector.

Although this opportunity had not been on my radar screen, I saw this as a great potential for growing my business. Because my existing brain trust counsel's expertise was strictly on the domestic level, I reached out to the International Franchise Council headquartered in Washington, DC. Thanks to this terrific organization, I found a brain trust advisor who had experience developing business relationships with Taiwanese and U.S.-based companies.

Whether you are an "intrapreneur" in a corporate environment or an "entrepreneur" ready to start and grow your own enterprise, recognize the importance of finding one or more brain trust advisors. If you are fortunate enough to be part of an organization that has provided you with a mentor or sponsor, congratulations. Figure out your goals, and then take the advice of your mentors and work on achieving them.

Four Tips for Choosing Brain Trust Advisors

1. Figure out what you want to accomplish. This will help you to determine the individual(s) you should ask to be part of your brain trust cabinet.

2. Begin by sending a formal letter or email to your choice of one or more of your potential brain trust advisors. Include information about your organization and explain why you would like the individual(s) to be your brain trust advisor. State the time commitment (once per quarter). A convenient location to meet the individual is also recommended.

3. Once the individual agrees, send a thank you along with proposed dates. One month before the date of your brain trust meeting, send a description of the situation about which you will be seeking advice.

4. Each time that you meet with your brain trust advisor, send a follow-up detailing what you gleaned from your meeting. Also, show how you intend to implement the recommended advice. During future meetings, share what worked as a direct result of the counsel from your brain trust advisor.

ACTION STEP: FIGURE OUT WHERE YOU WANT TO BE. THEN GIVE CAREFUL THOUGHT TO SELECTING A BRAIN TRUST ADVISOR WHO WILL GIVE YOU THE NECESSARY COUNSEL TO ACCOMPLISH YOUR GOAL.

They Have a Good Outlook on Life

Secret 29 for Creating Your Own Success: Stay Positive

When you are confronted with unexpected doom and gloom situations, do you react too negatively? Or do you feel that somehow "there's got to be a pony inside"? A common trait of self-made millionaires is maintaining a positive attitude no matter how dire the situation.

Being positive is a learned choice. It is an attitude.

Negative people often see unpleasant situations as unsolvable. Those with positive attitudes, however, see the same stressful situations in a different light. Rather than moping about what they have been confronted with, positive people consider alternate solutions for how the situation can be handled.

Positive people are "challenge-solvers" while negative people interpret stressful situations as "problems." Being positive expends less energy than being negative.

Self-made millionaires are definitely positive people. Perhaps that it why they are known for creating their own success. They snap out of "Why did it happen to me?" mode and instead focus on the bright side of things no matter how difficult the situation.

Though I have five secrets yet to master to achieve millionaire status, I am absolutely positive that "being positive" is a trait in my genes. In fact, I am such a Pollyanna that I often annoy people with my positive spirit.

I specifically remember two situations when my positivity even surprised me.

Situation One:

I had been wanting to replace my nine-year-old car but could not justify trading it in to buy a new one. One day, when driving my children to soccer practice, another car hit ours. The children were not hurt, nor were the people in the other car. I hit my head against the windshield and was taken to the hospital. As I waited in the emergency room for the x-ray results, the policeman writing the accident report came in and told me that my car had been totaled. Rather than being upset, my response to him was, "Enough for a BMW?" His response was, "Lady, are you crazy?" My response, "Possibly. They are checking to see if I have a concussion." The policeman would have been surprised: I did have a concussion—and, one week later, a red BMW.

Situation Two:

Another situation when being positive paid off remains in the forefront of my mind. It is what happened nine months after starting what is now my thirty-one-year-old consulting firm. I had three silent partners who owned 50 percent of the business. They informed me that they wanted "out." They did not see the business generating revenue fast enough, and their solution was to disband the company. I could have been livid with them. However, I saw their "wanting out" as an opportunity.

I brainstormed with a friend who happened to be an attorney. The proposed solution that we came up with was to buy out my three partners, paying them back what they had put into the business over a two-year period. After putting a "win-win" agreement in place, I realized that their wanting to get out of the business was a blessing in disguise. I recognized the benefits and saw that it would be much easier to support one person when growing the business rather than four.

Being positive paid off. Three months later, after spending nine months pitching a column, a Gannet newspaper picked up my weekly column. Two months later, I landed a $20,000 piece of business. And the best part was that I did not harbor any negative feelings toward my three former partners. I ended up hiring them as independent contractors two years later!

In the August 29, 2014, "Productivity" section of *Inc.* magazine, contributing editor Geoffrey James explains that your attitude defines and delimits your level of success. "If you have an upbeat attitude, you'll achieve at least some level of success. If you have a lousy attitude," Geoffrey writes, "you'll see obstacles as threats and annoyances. If you have a positive attitude, you'll see obstacles as interesting or even fun."[1]

I asked Steve Humble, the seventeenth self-made millionaire interviewed for this book, how a positive attitude made a difference in his life. He explained that it is easy to be positive when times are good; however, it is most beneficial when times are hard.

Steve shared that positive attitude was definitely challenged in 2008 when the economy collapsed. It was a difficult time for his organization, Creative Home Engineering. In fact, for a while he wasn't sure that his organization would survive. Obviously,

Steve certainly did not enjoy this unbelievably stressful and difficult predicament. The burden of supporting not only his family but also that of his employees was overwhelming.

When things were bleakest, however, Steve reminded himself that he had always been completely honest with his customers (despite many opportunities to do the opposite) and he knew that he was doing his very best. He cherished knowing that even if everything went badly, he would still have his integrity and reputation. That one glimmer of positivity transformed his way of thinking to more of a "come what may" kind of attitude that allowed him to climb out and succeed.

Steve Humble also shared the importance of a positive work environment. When starting Creative Home Engineering in 2004, one of his goals was to maintain a positive work environment. He focused on hiring people whom he liked to be around rather than those who had the most impressive resumes. That made it possible for him to attract other people who also placed a high value on a positive and pleasant work environment.

So as you see, being positive pays off. It also comes in handy when unexpected situations arise as Steve described.

Three Steps for Staying Positive

1. When confronted with a negative situation, evaluate how and why it occurred. If you were responsible for it happening, consider it a learning experience.

2. Talk about how you feel to someone—a positive person, that is—who is willing to listen rather than giving you "would have, should have, could have" advice. Oftentimes, it is easier to work through a dire situation when you have someone to bounce things off of.

3. Avoid displacing your aggression on someone else. Rather than pointing a finger, move on. Stay positive.

Action Step: Monitor the words that you use for one week. Every time you hear yourself use a negative word when speaking or writing, rephrase what you said using a positive one.

Secret 30 for Creating Your Own Success: Be Happy

In a July 6, 2015 *Observer* article by Benjamin Hardy, he writes, "Only one in three Americans say they are very happy."[2] Is happiness an easy-to-learn life skill or innate quality?

I strongly believe that happiness may be both! What I know for certain is that being happy is a mindset. It is a choice. It is how you allow yourself to react to things.

For instance, although it is only "human" to react to what is going on in your environment, people who are happy have the confidence not to allow people or situations to negatively affect their emotions. People who are content with themselves also have a positive effect on others. In fact, if you saw the movie *The Greatest Showman*, you might remember that P.T. Barnum said, "The noblest art in the world is making others happy." A happy person's positive emotions are contagious, which makes others want to be around them.

"Unhappy" people, on the other hand, often interpret people or situations as making them experience feeling sad, angry, and other negative emotions. What they do not recognize is that the unhappiness stems from how they choose to react to the situation rather than the situation itself.

A specific situation that occurs in the workplace is a manager recommending to a team member that a project should be handled differently than it is currently being managed. The employee may experience unhappiness by believing that his manager does not like his work. If the employee, however, would learn to take his manager's constructive criticism *professionally* rather than *personally*, the emotion of unhappiness would not be part of the workplace equation.

Dr. Zachary Berk, the eighteenth self-made millionaire in this book, holds the title of Chief Happiness Officer. He believes that happiness indeed can be learned. That is one reason that he started HappCo in 2014. His innovative software company combines technology, data, and service to help organizations know if their employees are happy and engaged.

Dr. Berk says that talents and human potential are the most important assets for a company's success. He also has found that when organization's managers know when their team members are happy or not, they can better manage them.

His organization has the tools to help companies and their people identify the happiness quotient of its employees. As a result, team members become more effective and happier about their work, themselves, and their contributions. Dr. Berk has found that the end result is improving a company's positive impact and ultimately the bottom line.

Dr. Berk and his team have found that when an organization invests in the series of HappCo's fun tools and assessments, the end result is to learn if their employees are feeling good. Although each employee's response is kept anonymous, the feedback provides their organizations with their level of happiness and engagement. Employees are also given a daily happiness tracker that gives management a day-to-day happiness tracking of their company.

Four Ways to Analyze How Happy a Person You Are

1. Write down the last time you considered yourself "happy." What was going on in your life that made you experience this emotion?

2. Write down the last time you were unhappy. What caused it and what did you do to overcome feeling that way?

3. Write down three experiences that make you feel the happiest. Schedule time this week to participate in one or more of them.

4. Write down the situations that make you feel the unhappiest. Make a point of eliminating these situations from your life one day at a time until you no longer experience them.

ACTION STEP: SMILE AT THREE PEOPLE TODAY. BESIDES MAKING THEM FEEL GOOD ABOUT THEMSELVES, YOU MAY EXPERIENCE A PERIPHERAL BENEFIT: A SMILE IN RETURN.

Secret 31 for Creating Your Own Success: Stay Motivated

What is the driving force that gets you out of bed in the morning? Is it your blaring alarm clock? Is it that cup of coffee waiting for you? Is it your kids counting on you to make them breakfast? Is it the job you love or perhaps the appointment that you have scheduled?

Whatever gets you going each day and keeps you psyched is called *motivation*. It is the force that guides your actions. The dictionary defines motivation as the reason(s) one has for acting in a certain way.

When first starting my consulting business, I learned that people are motivated in one of two ways: through either the "carrot effect" or through the "KITA effect." If you are not familiar with these forms of behavior modification, let me explain them to you.

The "carrot effect" refers to completing what you started knowing that there will be a positive incentive after the action is completed. For instance, if you are an hourly worker and you work overtime, you will be paid more money. The extra money is motivation to work more. Or if you book an airline flight a few months in advance, you may pay less than if you booked the flight two days before your departure date. Saving money is the motivating factor for booking a flight early.

On the other side of the motivation spectrum is what many people know as the "KITA effect." This acronym refers to the "kick in the tail approach."

Some people find the fear factor to be a good motivator. For instance, Serena Williams, the world famous American tennis player, has been quoted as saying, "Losing makes me even more motivated."[3]

It really does not matter what motivates you as much as staying motivated in the first place. One of the qualities that successful people have in common is their drive for what they want to do. One of the many factors that inspire individuals is to begin by setting specific goals. Their specificity is a motivating factor to help them work toward their goals. In order to stay motivated rather than overwhelmed as they are working toward their goal, successful people divide what needs to be done into smaller components. By doing so, most of them found it easier to remain motivated by completing parts of the project one step at a time rather than risking the thought of giving up.

More often than not, individuals who aspire to be successful become demotivated and do not finish what they started out to do. How different their end result could have been if they allowed themselves to achieve small successes by dividing a large project into smaller components.

What about you? What do you do to stay motivated? Do you divide a large project into smaller pieces before beginning it? How do you avoid the temptation to give up when you face a roadblock? Individuals who consistently finish what they begin find a way to keep themselves motivated all the way to the finish line.

For example, because you are still reading this book, I would venture to say that one of your goals is to achieve self-made millionaire status. If that is the case, then rather than attempting to implement the fifty-two secrets at the same time, your success rate will be higher—and you will stay more motivated—by writing down exactly what you want your end result to be. Then map out the specific amount of time that you will commit to completing each secret.

Once you are certain that you have made one of the fifty-two secrets part of your modus operandi, you will be motivated to begin the next secret. As the saying in Spanish goes, "Poco a poco, se va lejos" ("little by little, you go far").

Four Ways to Stay Motivated

1. Begin with the end in mind by figuring out what you want to accomplish.

2. Hold yourself accountable by writing down your intended goal.

3. Divide your goal into smaller parts and write down specific deadlines for when you will finish each component of your goal.

4. Acknowledge your progress each time you successfully complete a section. This will keep you motivated to continue to move forward with the remainder of your project.

Also be sure to check out the Motivational Monday website (*www.motivationalmonday.com*).

ACTION STEP: FIGURE OUT WHAT YOU WANT IN LIFE. THEN DETERMINE HOW YOU WILL MOTIVATE YOURSELF TO MAKE IT A REALITY.

Habit 14

They Take Initiative

Secret 32 for Creating Your Own Success: Challenge Yourself

Are you ready to stretch toward your fullest potential? Now that you are more than halfway finished with this book, I hope that you are getting psyched to put the fifty-two secrets for creating your own success into practice. Forgive me for putting the carriage before the horse; however, I am so excited that you are joining me on this journey.

Forward march to Secret 32. Let's start by figuring out the exact definition of the word *challenge*.

According to the Cambridge Dictionary, this term is described as "Something needing great mental or physical strength in order to be done successfully." I am sure that there has not been a shortage of challenges to overcome in your life. The good news about having faced your past challenges is that you will be better prepared to master Secret 32 for creating your own success.

Each of the individuals interviewed for this book successfully worked through the challenges that they faced in order to achieve their self-made millionaire status. Let me name a few:

Allan S. was challenged by what he could have interpreted as defeat the first time he auditioned for a violin position with the New York Philharmonic and was not given an offer. Instead, for two years, he challenged himself to improve his musical ability to play orchestral pieces before returning to audition once again with this world-renowned symphony orchestra. He found that putting himself up to the challenge paid off when he was offered a violin chair.

Sarian Bouma challenged herself when she was at the lowest point in her life by not having enough food stamps to buy milk for her newborn. Rather than giving up, she challenged herself to figure out a way to create a better life. And that Sarian did. After learning marketable business skills and finding a job, she began her own business. She taught her more than two hundred employees how to challenge themselves to take control of their lives.

And then there is Nick Kovacevich. It sounds to me like this entrepreneur has been challenging himself since the day he was born. Besides graduating magna cum laude from Southwest Baptist University and being captain of the nationally ranked men's basketball team, Nick achieved his self-made millionaire status at the age of twenty-seven. This accomplished pioneer in the emerging legal cannabis industry shared that he continues to challenge himself by raising his goals based on the opportunities in front of him—or, better said, that he creates. A perfect example of the way Nick is presently challenging himself is by setting the next goal for his company, Kush Bottles: to get to $100M in annual revenue, $10M in annual profit with a $10 price per share, and one hundred employees. You can see that Nick is up for the challenge.

Now that you read how the these three individuals challenged themselves to achieve self-made millionaire status, it is your turn.

Think about the last time you challenged yourself into doing something that took great mental or physical strength. Perhaps it was when you committed to a weekly exercise regime. Maybe it was when you were up for that promotion and challenged yourself to convince your manager that you were the most qualified person for the job. Or was it when you were asked to complete a project without ample notice and were challenged with the short amount of time that you had to complete it? Perhaps you began the business and were challenged about how to manage cash flow?

Whether your past challenges were large or small, the way in which you successfully managed them prepared you to handle the ones that you will continue to face. Each challenge that you successfully manage gives you the confidence to face future ones. As you prepare to become a self-made millionaire, challenge yourself by setting your expectations higher. Not only will you accomplish more, you also will be up for the next challenge that is just around the corner.

Three Ways to Prepare for Challenges

1. Write down the greatest challenge that you have overcome. Describe what you did to manage it.

2. When you are faced with life's next challenge, remind yourself how you have handled past ones. Your past successes will give you the confidence to handle future hurdles.

3. Recognize that, if you are not confronted with challenges in life, you may not be living life to its fullest. Though the

challenges that you create should not be unrealistic, they should be large enough for you to create a new learning opportunity and way of thinking.

Action Step: Challenge yourself on an intellectual level by reading about a new topic. Challenge yourself emotionally by expressing your feelings. Challenge yourself physically by creating or expanding your exercise regime. Challenge yourself on a spiritual level by listing the people, experiences, and things for which you are grateful.

Secret 33 for Creating Your Own Success: Ask Until You Get a Yes

Successful people know the power of persuasion. They interpret *no* as meaning, *not now, not the right time,* or *too busy to make a decision.* They ask the same question more than once and at different times to get the answer they want.

Those individuals on the receiving end may get annoyed by the pursuit. Based on the style of being asked, the person may actually respect the creativity of the person asking the same question multiple times. The difference is in the style of asking.

Some people enjoy the chase as much the catch. Which one are you?

James Timothy White, the twentieth self-made millionaire in this book, who achieved this seven-digit status at the age of sixteen, certainly enjoys both the chase and the catch. At age twelve, he founded his first company in Canada, which he grew into a multi-million-dollar corporate structure. In 2005, he sold the business and set out to pursue a promising new venture in finance.

Like many successful entrepreneurs, James picked himself up from bankruptcy and convinced his family into investing in his next venture, which led him to become the world's youngest CEO of a publicly traded company on the Frankfurt Stock Exchange.

When James was seventeen years old, he had a very small business. He received a call from a large engineering company called SNC Lavalin Nexacor that had several hundred towers through the province of Alberta in Canada, called the Alberta Supernet. The property manager had found James through the website he had built and asked if was interested in bidding on a contract to maintain the towers, including snow removal in the winter and landscaping in the summer. Without giving it a second thought, James asked that the necessary paperwork be emailed to him to bid the project.

That night, after receiving the bid packages, this teen showed the paperwork to his mom and explained that he was going to bid on these sites across Alberta. She vehemently said no, that he could not do it. Although he knew his mom was right, James would not take no for an answer!

James bid the project, not realizing that he was the only bidder on the contract and, by default, he won. Although his mom was against it, both she and James's dad supported him as he moved forward with this undertaking.

In fact, his dad drove him to a Ford dealership to purchase a few trucks. At eighteen years old and with a limited credit history, his application was declined. James turned a *no* into a *yes* once again by asking to speak with the dealership owner. After a few minutes of talking to the owner and explaining the contract he had won, the owner asked that James return to the dealership with his dad the following day. Within a few days, James had finance approval to buy brand new F250 diesel pickup trucks with snow plows. It was, however, a form of creative financing: The owner of the dealership used his own money to finance James's purchases.

So now with plows, the trucks, the blowers, and shovels, James had no idea where to find staff. At eighteen years old, his parents quit their jobs to work with their son. The only problem was he had no money because all of it was used to gear up for the new contract.

The company was on ninety-days-payable terms, which meant it took three months to get their first check. James's mom and dad remortgaged their house. They also maxed out their credit cards in order for him to pay for gas, lodging, and insurance. By the end of the year, James received a check for the contract. That gave him enough money to pay off the mortgage and the credit cards.

Fast-forward to 2006. His parents purchased the company, then consolidated it by selling the divisions that were not as favorable (landscaping, courier, asset management, and so on). At this point, the company's sole focus is operating as a heavy-duty truck and trailer repair shop, which has become one of the largest in the city and which currently occupies a 17,000 square foot shop.

If James had taken no for an answer, he and his parents would all be miserable working dead-end jobs.

Today, James's primary focus is building his Florida-wide real estate company (WeSaySold.com) and managing various investments (BinaryBiometrics.com) and (DrugTestingCourses.com). James also takes pride in helping other established small businesses grow by using his own capital in order for hard-working small businesspeople to purchase equipment, update technology, and improve processes and procedures through automation.

Four Steps for Turning a No Into a Yes

1. Ask yourself why your request is so important to you. Write down the benefits.

2. Timing is everything. Schedule time when the person you are asking can give you his or her full attention.

3. Recognize if you get a "no" to your request the first time, you must prepare to rephrase your request. If the person being asked is adamant about not agreeing to your request, ask if you could discuss it again in a few months. Then send an email follow-up to the person to thank them for his or her time and share that you will follow up with then in a few months, as discussed.

4. Follow up by the promised time and follow through. Remember that the term *if* does not exist in the vocabulary of successful people. It is a matter of *when*!

ACTION STEP: THE NEXT TIME SOMEONE IN YOUR PERSONAL OR PROFESSIONAL LIFE SAYS NO TO YOUR REQUEST, RECOGNIZE THAT GETTING THE ANSWER YOU WANT IS A PROCESS. ASK THE SAME QUESTION OVER A PERIOD OF TIME UNTIL YOU GET A *YES*.

Secret 34 for Creating Your Own Success: Create Your Own Luck

It takes more than the luck of the Irish to be successful. A big part of being lucky is your mindset and how you react to situations.

Tennessee Williams's words prove it: "Luck is believing you're lucky."[1] Could a positive attitude be an essential trait of "lucky" people?

I know for a fact that being lucky is the way you react to situations. It is an attitude.

People with positive attitudes use their creativity to work to their benefit. I remember a particular situation in which rejection was right around the corner from me. Because I despise the word *no,* I decided to put my creative juices to work.

It was January 1989 and I had pitched a "Business Manners" weekly column to the *Dayton Daily News.* Alan Kelly was the editor of this particular newspaper and indicated that he saw the value of my column for his readers. He told me that they were also considering another person who had pitched a column about a similar topic. I sent him several sample columns and then called him twice a month to learn when they would be making their decision.

By the first week of March, Mr. Kelly told me that he and his team were on the verge of making a decision and my column was their second choice!

At that point, I decided to "try my luck" at enticing them to make my column their first choice by putting my creativity into practice. My goal was to strike a nerve—positive, of course—with this editor of Irish background. And because St. Patrick's Day was right around the corner, the timing, it seemed, was perfect!

I bought bright green stationery with a matching envelope and sent a letter to this Irishman that read, "It takes more than the luck of the Irish to be successful in business today. I hope you will let me assist you in giving your readers that competitive edge through my Business Manners column." I then signed the letter, "Ann Marie O'Sabath—just for today."

This action may sound like a silly thing to do, but guess what? It worked!

I created my own luck. My weekly column became their first pick and it ran in their section for four years!

Successful people create their own success. They see "opportunities" in situations that others may perceive as losing propositions. These people who supposedly "create their own luck" operate from a place of confidence. They convert a mere thought, a good deed, and even a misfortune into an opportunity. They are the people who put their "create your own luck" into practice along with the other fifty-one secrets for creating their own success. They are the people who become self-made millionaires.

Mickey Redwine, the twenty-first self-made millionaire in this book, is one of them. He achieved his millionaire status at age thirty-six. Many of Mickey's competitors attribute his success to "being lucky." Mickey is the first to agree with them—if you know how to create your own luck, that is! And he sure does!

CNBC defines Mickey as a pioneer in fiberoptics who was in the trenches during the internet boom. His company, Dynamic Holdings, was responsible for laying thousands of miles of fiber optic cable throughout the country.

Like other "lucky" people, Mickey is intentional with his life decisions. He interjects only positive and absolute conditions in his life that are within his control. Mickey shared that when people stop creating planned and structured positive outcomes for their future, by default their lives are subject to happenstance—the antithesis of "creating your own luck." Among Mickey's secrets for being lucky is the law of attraction as advocated by one of his favorite authors, Rhonda Byrne, who wrote *The Secret* and *The Magic.*

Here are six strategies that Mickey Redwine recommends for *you* to create your own luck:

1. Maintain a positive "I will do it" mindset. Although raised in a tin house, Mickey shared that he knew from a very young age that he would achieve success.

2. Play by your own rules. Follow Mickey Redwine's strategy by *negotiating* contracts rather than bidding them.

3. Create yourself and your business to be what your customers want, need, and expect. Then exceed their expectations. Give them "lagniappe," an old Louisiana tradition, especially in the French Quarter of New Orleans. It means thanking customers in some way for their patronage.

4. Do good deeds. Pay it forward each and every day. Besides living the "pay it forward" principle, Mickey helps those in need through mentorship by giving individuals the encouragement and knowledge to succeed in life.

5. Focus on re-creating a *fortune* when you are confronted with *misfortune*. Everyone encounters some level of misfortune in life. Mickey knows about misfortune. He lost nearly everything during the WorldCom scandal. Barely avoiding bankruptcy, he did what he does best: He picked himself up once again and rebuilt his fortune. Now if that is not creating your own luck, what is?

6. Be diligent, thankful, and appreciative, and you *will* create your own luck! Design and put into place circumstances that are favorable and conducive to your own specific goals. Once you have done that, you are destined to succeed. Recognize the opportunities that you have set in motion and seize them with a passion.

Three More Ways to Make "Luck" Work for You

1. Take a chance. Whether it is being the first to jump-start a conversation or reacting to a situation that does not appear to be going as you expected, take control. That is when creating your own luck will begin!

2. Be open to new experiences. Sometimes a random action is what will guide you to "creating your own luck." Rather than being disappointed that something has not gone your way, shift your thinking by seeing it as an opportunity.

3. Spin the wheel of success. Take that chance. That is often how luck begins!

ACTION STEP: THE NEXT TIME SOMETHING DOES NOT GO YOUR WAY, CREATE YOUR OWN LUCK.

They Are Imaginative

Secret 35 for Creating Your Own Success: Make It Happen

Self-made millionaires are without question "make it happen" people!

Which one are you? A "want to make it happen" person? A "wish it could happen" person? Or a "make it happen" person?

A *Want to Make It Happen* Person

When was the last time you had an idea that you wanted to make happen, yet didn't? Perhaps you allowed perceived roadblocks to stand in the way. Or the people in your life told you that your "want to make it happen" idea was a ridiculous thought? Or you were reminded of the last idea you had that failed?

Unfortunately, *want to make it happen* people may not realize that a key ingredient for succeeding is to surround themselves with *make it happen* people. Instead of moving forward with the idea, the slightest words of discouragement, self-doubt, or past failures keep *want to make it happen* people from moving forward when their idea could be the best invention since Thomas Edison's light bulb. And if they had read Secret 20 (Turn Failures Into Opportunities), they would have learned that Edison failed thirty-one times before he *made it happen!*

When I look back on starting what is now my thirty-one-year-old consulting business, I realize that I was fortunate to be surrounded with other business owners who were *make it happen* people. With their words of encouragement and knowledge, I did not give a second thought to wondering if I could make it happen. Perhaps I should have been more scared of starting a business (and on a shoestring budget, nonetheless), but I wasn't. The main reason was because I had surrounded myself with successful business owners. Their knowledge for getting through the growing pains of starting a business gave me the confidence to *make it happen.*

A *Wish It Could Happen* Person

If you are a *wish it could happen* person, you may spend more time dreaming about doing something than actually figuring out *how* to make it happen.

At one point in my life, I was a *wish it could happen* person. What changed me from being a *wish it could happen* person to becoming a *make it happen* person was reading the following phrase: "If you were ninety-two, what would you wish you would have done?"

That question really made me think. Hmmm. Well, I wanted to start a business. Check. I was in the midst of that. I wanted to have enough East Coast clients to support an office in New York.

I wasn't sure how I was going to make that happen, so I put the goal on my "bucket list." I soon realized that believing that I could do it was an essential second ingredient to *making it happen.*

Five years later, after believing that I could do it, networking like mad, and executing a master marketing plan to convert East Coast prospects into clients, I finally had enough business to open an office in New York City. I had transitioned from a *wish it could happen* person to joining the *make it happen* league.

I know one thing is certain: So can you! Stop wishing and devise a plan to *make it*—whatever you want—*happen!*

A *Make It Happen* Person

Did you know that a major factor for *make it happen* people is their belief in themselves? I have always believed that the worst disease in the world is not cancer, is not Alzheimer's, is not heart failure—or any other of the diseases we often hear about. I truly believe that the worst disease in the world is the lack of self-esteem.

You do not have to be the smartest game in town to make something happen. You simply have to believe in yourself enough to know that you can do it.

When I was in my early thirties, I was teaching. My children had just started school, and I was ready to transition from the world of teaching to the business sector. The challenge was that I did not know how to do it.

When I was in search of an answer, I would head to the bookstore to find a relevant book on the particular topic. In this case, I found the book *How to Get Anything You Want.* I bought it and marched home to find the answer. I was so naive that I read it cover to cover beginning with the first page. If I had been savvy, I would have saved myself time by reading the last page first.

Let me save you time from reading the book and telling you how to get anything you want out of life. Are you ready? *Do whatever it takes to make it happen* (an age-old mantra of *make it happen* people!).

~~~

So if you are a *want to make it happen* person or a *wish it could happen* person, you now have the know-how to become a *make it happen* person.

The Three Steps for Becoming a **Make It Happen** *Person*

1. Figure out what you want and devise a plan for getting there. Give yourself a deadline.

2. Surround yourself with individuals who have already accomplished your intended goal. A support system is essential to give you both the confidence and "know-how" to succeed.

3. Get ready to *make it happen!* If you do not know of someone who has accomplished what you want to make happen, I am sure that there is a book on the topic. If not, then figure out how to do it and make writing that book on your future to-do list.

Get ready, get set, *make it happen!* In order to do so, take self-made millionaire Dru Riess's advice: "You've got to put everything aside, people doubting you, people saying, 'that's not a good idea,' and just. . .grind through that. Push through it." As a result of starting Popular Ink in McKinney, Texas, he became a self-made millionaire in his mid-twenties. In 2016 Popular Ink generated $25 million in sales. The company now has fifty-one full-time employees. Dru made it happen. So can you!

ACTION STEP: FIGURE OUT WHAT YOU WANT TO ACCOMPLISH. THEN WRITE IT DOWN TO MAKE YOUR "WANT" A REALITY. FINALLY, SURROUND YOURSELF WITH PEOPLE WHO HAVE ALREADY *MADE IT HAPPEN!*

Secret 36 for Creating Your Own Success: The Sky Is the Limit

Successful people live within boundaries—their own, that is. They create time boundaries. They create money management boundaries. They create boundaries by setting defined goals.

The one place where successful people do not set boundaries is for developing their potential to its fullest. They expand their thinking by going past their existing experiences in order to create their own reality of possibilities. They increase their odds by figuring out what they want and then working to accomplish it. These individuals develop and maintain the mindset that "the sky is the limit."

This is especially true with first-generation Americans. In fact, according to quora.com, one in three U.S. millionaires are foreign-born or first-generation American.[1] And 80 percent of these individuals are self-made millionaires who have instilled in themselves the confidence and mindset that the sky *is* the limit.

Shama Hyder, the twenty-third self-made millionaire in this book, achieved this status at twenty-seven years of age after moving from India to the United States at the age of nine. She shared that it was the power of the mind and pure determination that helped her to turn an unfamiliar situation into a comfortable one. Her "want" to be the best she could be in a foreign environment allowed her to thrive in a new school with new friends and a new culture.

Besides her pure determination, this high achiever remained open to new ideas, new people, and new ways of thinking. As a result, Shama acquired the limitless belief that she could achieve anything that she set her mind to do. When asked what accomplishing her self-made millionaire goal did for her, she said, "It made me realize there was nothing I couldn't achieve once I set my mind to it. The sky became the limit!"

Shama shared that the "sky is the limit" way of thinking also played a vital role for growing The Marketing Zen Group, her global online marketing and digital PR company. She is also the author of *The Zen of Social Media Marketing: An Easier Way to Build Credibility, Generate Buzz and Increase Revenue.*

Five Ways to Adopt a Growth Mindset to Make the Sky Your Limit

1. Buy a plant and think of it as the thought that you want to develop.

2. Place it near light according to the plant directions. Put yourself in a similar situation by scheduling time to be with people who give you growth stimulation based on what they have accomplished and what you want to achieve.

3. Each day feed the plant with water, fertilizer, or natural light. Do the same with your mind by reading about accomplished individuals who stimulate your growth mindset.

4. As the plant grows, replant it in a larger pot. Do the same by expanding your activities to develop your growth potential.

5. Continue this growth mindset by doing one activity each day to grow your thought into a reality. Use the plant's growth as a gauge for your own "the sky is the limit" development.

ACTION STEP: RECOGNIZE THAT YOU CAN HAVE ANYTHING YOU WANT WHEN YOU PUT YOUR MIND TO IT. CREATE A "THE SKY IS THE LIMIT" MINDSET.

Habit 16

They Innovate

Secret 37 for Creating Your Own Success: Reinvent Yourself

Everyone has a self-made millionaire in their midst. They are often so understated, however, that their family and friends may not even recognize that they gradually reinvent themselves.

How do they reinvent themselves? By moving forward each time they recognize an opportunity that others may dismiss. They continually better themselves by what they read. They make a point of learning "what to do" and "what not to do" from people with whom they choose to spend time.

This book would not be complete without Jim Abraham, who I am writing about as the twenty-fourth self-made millionaire. Uncle Jim was my mother's brother. Although few if anyone noticed, Uncle Jim reinvented himself several times over the years. He began by sweeping floors in a restaurant, working in a popcorn stand, and then dipping turtles in chocolate in a restaurant that he eventually bought.

Although he has since passed, I would like to share with you how this man reinvented himself for more than four decades. These gradual reinventions allowed him to become a self-made millionaire in his sixties by investing in real estate.

Uncle Jim had a great work ethic. He was born into a Syrian immigrant family who came to the United States in 1914. I remember my mom telling me that her and Uncle Jim's parents were so poor that on Christmas morning, their gifts would be an orange and pair of socks in their stockings.

When Uncle Jim was seven years old, he and two of his friends were playing in an alley next to a candy store. Mr. Mischka, the candy store owner, was putting trash in garbage cans in the alley and asked the three of them, "Would any of you like to have a job doing chores for me a few days a week?" Uncle Jim immediately said yes. Although he did it to earn money, what he may not have realized is that *he was at the beginning of his journey to reinvent himself!* With his parents' permission, he worked in the candy store after school a few days a week for nine years.

In order to help provide for his family, Uncle Jim quit school and asked Mr. Mischka if he could have more hours. *Reinvention!* Mr. Mischka not only gave him extra hours, he also invested in a popcorn stand to place in front of the candy store with Uncle Jim's name painted on it. Another reinvention!

Besides paying him an hourly wage, Mr. Mischka gave Uncle Jim 50 percent of the revenue from his popcorn sales. *Reinvention!* Two years later, World War II broke out. Uncle Jim enlisted in the Army and said goodbye to his family, friends, Mr. Mischka, and his popcorn stand. *Reinvention!*

In 1944, he returned to Amherst, Ohio. Uncle Jim went to see Mr. Mischka, who welcomed him with open arms to return to work at the candy store. This time, however, he learned about how to run the business. *Reinvention!*

He arrived early to open the store. He also learned how to make chocolate-covered dates and caramel turtles as well as wait on customers. *Reinvention!*

Two years later, Mr. Mischka asked Uncle Jim if he would like to buy the candy store. He was thrilled and could not believe how "lucky" he was to have this opportunity. Uncle Jim and Mr. Mischka worked out a monetary arrangement that was financially agreeable for both of them.

One holiday season, there were so many out-of-town candy shipping requests that when the season was over, Uncle Jim realized that he had established a mail-order business for his candy. *Reinvention!* He had generated $20,000 in 1948 (equivalent to $206,000 by today's standards).

Uncle Jim's lawyer friend said to him, "Jimmy, if you want to be wealthy, invest in a piece of land." Later that year, he took $20,000 from the candy business and purchased several acres of farmland. *Reinvention!* His land investments continued every few years until he was no longer known as the man who owned Mischka's. He was the man who owned a lot of real estate!

Decades later, Uncle Jim, who you probably feel that you know by now, was approached by a commercial development company. They offered to buy some of his land for a shopping center development. He did not sell them the land. Instead he leased it to them and remained the landowner. *Reinvention!*

Three Ways to Reinvent Yourself

1. Write down what you have accomplished to date for moving forward or reinventing yourself. Perhaps it was relocating, earning a degree, changing jobs, meeting individuals who you consider mentors, and so forth.

2. Write down your five-year, ten-year, and fifteen-year goals. Next to them, write down how you need to reinvent yourself in order to achieve them.

3. Each time you achieve a new reinvention milestone, congratulate yourself. Your positive mindset will keep you moving forward.

ACTION STEP: BASED ON THE SKILLS YOU HAVE DEVELOPED, WHAT CAN YOU DO TO REINVENT YOURSELF IN ORDER TO ACCOMPLISH YOUR OWN SELF-MADE MILLIONAIRE STATUS?

Secret 38 for Creating Your Own Success: Embrace Change

Henry Ford knew what he was saying when he said, "If you always do what you've always done, you'll always get what you've always got."

Self-made millionaires are quite good at coping with change. In fact, many of them actually thrive on it. Rather than questioning a changing situation, they figure out what caused it and then they move forward by creating a proposed solution. Their way of coping with change is much different from that of individuals who get stuck by making an effort to undo what cannot be changed.

Joe Palko, the twenty-fifth self-made millionaire interviewed for this book, became a millionaire at age twenty-five. He and his business partner, Scott Sanfilippo co-founded the *www.theferretstore.com*, an e-Commerce pet-supply retail company in 2000. Six years later they were one of the leading pet supply distributors in the United States. In 2006, The Ferret Store was sold to Drs. Foster and Smith.

Joe attributes embracing change as an important component to their success. Although their business was profitable in 2000, they saw that the margins in their six-year-old online business began slipping. They recognized that the difference was they had online competitors who had access to the same products that they did. Joe and Scott also noticed that their competitors were willing to sell items at or below cost just to increase their market share.

That is when these two entrepreneurs embraced change by developing their own pet food and pet accessories. Their brands were far more unique and of better quality than anything that could be purchased in a pet store. If they had not accepted the change that they saw on the horizon, Joe shared that their sales would have continued to decrease. Fortunately, their pet food was a huge success.

In any industries, to include the pet industry, customers are often very loyal to brands. Establishing a quality food brand guaranteed recurring orders for the life of the pet, and sometimes for the life of the customer.

Three Ways to Embrace Change

1. When you face a change in your professional life, ask yourself what the benefits will be. By focusing on the positive, the fear factor will lessen.

2. Schedule time to discuss the change with individuals who are comfortable reacting to change. A brainstorming session often dispels hesitation to a new way of doing things.

3. Reflect on the last time you were confronted with change and had no choice but to embrace it. Write down the benefits that occurred. This exercise will encourage you to have a positive mindset for changes that you will face in the future.

ACTION STEP: THE NEXT TIME YOU ARE INTRODUCED TO A CHANGE, EMBRACE IT.

Habit 17

They Have Self-Respect

Secret 39 for Creating Your Own Success: Be Respectful

Self-made millionaires place a high value on being respectful. It is a reflection of their character. Like everyone else, these successful people gain respect in one way: by earning it.

Gary M., a prominent attorney and the twenty-sixth self-made millionaire interviewed for this book, explained the way he demonstrates his respect for others is by making friends with all persons who he deals with in life. His sincere caring for people is exemplified in the eleven forms of respect that he extends to others. There is no hoo-ha here. I have personally witnessed it.

1. If he says he is going to do something, you can count on him doing it. (Secret 8: Keep Your Word)

2. He is honest. (Secret 9: Be a Person of Integrity)

3. When something is requested of him, my experience has been that he places as high a value on others' time as he does on his own time. (Secret 11: Be Punctual)

4. He lends an ear, which may be one of the reasons that individuals gravitate to him (Secret 22: Listen Up)

5. He is in front of the line when it comes to doing favors for others. (Secret 24: Pay It Forward)

6. He works out regularly, which demonstrates a respect for his physical appearance. (Secret 25: Exercise for the Health of It)

7. He respects his mind by scheduling time to meditate. (Secret 26: Take Time to Think)

8. He innately sees the good in people because he is optimistic by nature. (Secret 29: Stay Positive)

9. Having achieved his self-made millionaire status, he does not see himself as better than anyone else. (Secret 40: Be Humble)

10. He is appreciative of even the smallest favors extended, especially because he is usually the giver and not the receiver. (Secret 41: Be Grateful)

11. He helps others in need. (Secret 43: Give Back)

You may be saying to yourself, "I have those 11 attributes, yet I am not a self-made millionaire." Congratulations! I told you at the beginning of this book that you may be closer to self-made millionaire status than you think. It is a matter of keeping your eye on the big picture as you complete the remaining secrets in the book that are still on your "to do" list.

Five Ways to Show Respect to Others

1. Make everyone's request your priority. You can do this by under-promising and over-delivering.

2. Be more interested in learning about others than you share about yourself.

3. After listening to what someone has to say, echo what you heard before sharing your comments.

4. Anytime it takes someone more than fifteen minutes to do something for you, send them a follow-up note. The style of note (an e-note, keyed letter, or handwritten note) is your choice.

5. Treat everyone with a high level of courtesy. Your respect for others will demonstrate the respect that you have for yourself.

ACTION STEP: TREAT OTHERS WITH RESPECT TO SHOW OTHERS YOUR GOOD CHARACTER.

Secret 40 for Creating Your Own Success: Be Humble

One of the many preconceived notions that I had of self-made millionaires is that their success went to their head. Was I ever wrong! At least that has not been the case with the thirty self-made millionaires who are part of this book.

Although their net worth has changed, most self-made millionaires' values have not. They have a virtue that is often both overlooked and definitely underrated. It is their humility.

Perhaps the modest beginning of many of these individuals is one reason that they are low-key about their status despite their seven-figure net worth. Like many of us, they undoubtedly have put in the long hours to achieve their success. Some still do despite having "made it."

Now that they have achieved this success status, they have proven to themselves that they can do it. A large percentage of these individuals who have made it do not have the need or want, however, to flaunt their success or to be treated more special than anyone else. In fact, many self-made millionaires prefer to blend in. That is reflected by where they live, the vehicles some drive, and their modest dress. They choose to live below their means, as you will read in Secret 44 for creating your own success.

Warren Buffett is a prime example. Although *Fortune*'s 2017 list of the world's wealthiest billionaires ranked him the second-richest person on earth, Warren chooses to live in a home in Omaha, Nebraska, that he bought in 1958 valued at $31,500. His financial status has since changed, but, like many self-made individuals, his choice of creature comforts has stayed the same.

Besides living a modest life style in comparison to their net worth, these confident individuals also often prefer to remain under the radar screen in other ways. Many of them are the listeners of the world and prefer to focus more on others rather than bragging about their own accomplishments—unless asked, that is. They thrive on helping others to achieve success.

What about you? Why not test your humility quotient by taking the following four-point test:

1. You focus on others more than yourself.

2. You engage in conversations as an active listener by asking questions rather than sharing information about yourself.

3. You let your values take you down the right path rather than what may be in your best interests.

4. You enjoy giving even more than receiving.

How did you do? If you answered *yes* to the above questions, then you have this secret mastered. If not, practice makes perfect.

Four Ways to Stay Humble

1. Whether you are well on your way to achieving self-made millionaire status or are still on the journey, remember your roots. It will keep you from allowing your success-in-the-making or perhaps your achieved "success" from inflating your ego.

2. Focus on others. Ask more questions about others than what you share about yourself. Besides giving others an outlet to express themselves, you may be pleasantly surprised how much you will learn.

3. Help others in need. Besides making the world a better place, you will appreciate what you have even more.

4. When you are part of a team project, deemphasize your role in it. Instead, showcase others' contributions. Your modesty will take you far.

ACTION STEP: FOCUS ON OTHERS.

They Are Appreciative

Secret 41 for Creating Your Own Success: Be Grateful

In addition to Finding Your Passion, Embracing Change, Maintaining a Strong Work Ethic, and the other forty-eight secrets for creating your own success, another important practice for accomplishing self-made millionaire status is *being grateful*. I was surprised how important this secret was for the individuals interviewed for this book.

In his book *The 7 Core Skills of Everyday Happiness,* author Scott Wilhite says that being grateful and displaying happiness are the single greatest skills that you can have in your life. His favorite 10 words are "You can't be grateful and unhappy at the same time."[1]

Besides being happy, studies have proven that people who display their gratefulness are positive people. They focus on what they have rather than what they are lacking. They display their appreciation to others for even the smallest deed rendered. This is the true definition of being thankful.

Individuals who are appreciative have a passion for life. They start their day with an attitude of gratitude. Though it is easy to take a good life for granted, several of the self-made millionaires interviewed for this book shared that they make a point of reminding themselves for what they have to be thankful.

This attitude of gratitude is put into practice throughout the day by thanking a team member for a job well done, expressing appreciation to a customer for his business, displaying appreciation for a complaint, paying a compliment to another, and thanking a family member for not using a cell phone during dinner. By accentuating the positive through these acts of gratitude, the environment of these individuals becomes a more pleasant place to live and work. In addition, the individuals receiving these acknowledgments feel appreciated.

Being grateful is in contrast to expending energy on what is lacking in life. Successful people accentuate what they do have and what is working. They do not allow themselves to experience resentment when negative situations come their way. Instead, these successful people condition themselves to interpret a negative situation as a wake-up call and then learn from it. In other words, they maintain a positive attitude even when things are not going as they expected.

A misconception of self-made millionaires is that they are materialistic people. Although these individuals have indeed earned the right to live the life of luxury, what individuals looking at these people from the "outside in" may not realize is the life of abundance that these individuals extend to others. Their spiritual richness stems from their appreciation and gratitude for what they have that money cannot buy (such as their family and good health) as well as the gratification they receive by being able to give to others.

No matter how gratefulness is displayed, it ultimately turns into a form of abundant living for the giver based on the sincere appreciation extended to others. There is a spiritual law of life that says "What you focus on tends to grow." When you focus on being grateful for what you have, what you are thankful for tends to grow. This law of nature is called the law of abundance.

Another trait that goes hand in glove with these positive people is their glass is "completely full" mindset rather than having a "half-full" mindset. Whereas most people are not able to see the good in negative situations, self-made millionaires have conditioned themselves to do so. They teach themselves to be grateful for even negative situations because they see those as lessons to be learned. This is also the differentiator between the people who succeed in getting what they want out of life and those who succumb to failure rather than seeing it as a learning experience.

How would you rate your "being grateful" mindset with even the most negative situations? Let's say the last time you got a traffic ticket for driving over the speed limit? Faux pas!

At the risk of sounding like a Pollyanna, let me share my attitude of gratitude the last time I got a speeding ticket. Approximately twenty years ago, I was driving down a freeway listening to a song on one of my favorite radio stations. No excuse, however, without realizing it, I was driving fifteen miles over the speed limit. Before long, I noticed a police car with flashing lights behind my car. I got the message and pulled over to the side of the road.

When the police officer got out of his car and came up to mine, he asked if I realized I was speeding. I told him that I did not realize it and thanked him for stopping me. It was not a sarcastic thank you. It was not a "let me try to schmooze my way out of getting a ticket thank you." My "thank you" was a sincere one. I was annoyed with myself for going over the speed limit, though I was grateful to the police officer who had stopped me. He was simply doing his job. Although it was an expensive lesson for being more aware of changing speed limits on a freeway, my attitude of gratitude was appreciating that the officer was enforcing driving safety.

People who practice being grateful for what they have been given in their lives draw more good things to them. And I do not mean more traffic tickets. I mean a greater awareness to appreciate "the positive" in both the good and the unexpected happenings of life.

When she and her husband achieved self-made millionaire status, Bunny Lightsey, the twenty-seventh self-made millionaire interviewed for this book, said, "It made me realize how much God has blessed me."

Three Ways to Practice Being Grateful

1. Begin a gratitude journal. Write down what you have in your life for which you are grateful. Include both people as well as things.

2. Verbally acknowledge the people in your life who you wrote in your journal. Jot an e-note or handwritten note to those whose have affected your life that day. Your words will be appreciated.

3. Charity begins on the home and work fronts. It is easy to take the people closest to you for granted. Be grateful to family and colleagues daily. Let them know how much you appreciate the emotional, intellectual, spiritual, and physical support that they give to you.

ACTION STEP: EACH DAY, DOCUMENT THREE THINGS FOR WHICH YOU ARE GRATEFUL.

Secret 42 for Creating Your Own Success: Place a High Value on Your Personal Life

The self-made millionaires who I interviewed appeared to place a high value on their personal lives. Many of them shared that their families were the driving forces for them to work hard to achieve success.

Some of them came from humble beginnings. Perhaps that is why one of their strongest motivating factors was to give their families a better life than they had growing up.

In order to create successful businesses (or to climb the ranks if they were in the private sector), these self-made million-aires *and* their families made many sacrifices. Oftentimes, the breadwinner(s) worked sixty-hour to one-hundred-hour work weeks in order to do whatever it took to succeed. As a result, their spouses and children spent time without that family member.

I had the pleasure of visiting with each of the thirty individuals in person, by phone, or via email. Oftentimes, in-person or phone visits were not possible the first time around. I found that I was not competing with their trip to the Riviera. Rather, what was taking precedence was the commitments they had made to be with their families. Talk about refreshing! Here are a few of their responses:

"I apologize, but the kiddos and I are decorating our garage for a massive holiday party we are throwing this weekend. I look forward to linking up with you soon."

"I am taking my kids to Chicago on Friday and will be unavail-able to talk. Are you available the following week, either Tues., Oct. 3 or Wed., Oct. 4?"

No matter what their net worth, their personal life appears to prevail. Their "personal and family time" becomes the ultimate currency for their happiness. Steve S., the twenty-eighth self-made millionaire in this book, shared that throughout his career he continued to live consistent with providing for his family without compromising his personal values.

Now that Steve S. and the other twenty-nine self-made millionaires have "made it," their focus has become a balanced lifestyle rather than being a slave to making more money. Though they have not lost their drive and are still active in their businesses (unless retired), their financial freedom gives them the comfort to enjoy what money cannot buy: family time. They recognize that spending quality time with their families helps to create memories and traditions that will live on with their future generations.

Here is how some of these individuals described the benefit of their seven-figure success:

"Success allows me to give my time and money at a higher level—starting with my family. In the early years of Phillips Home Improvement, I didn't take vacations. Because of my success, I have been able to provide for my family, build meaningful family time into my schedule, and create lifelong memories. You cannot put a price tag on that!" —Jason Phillips

"I now have enough to raise and enrich my family. Enough to play. Enough to house and feed friends and family and the occasional traveler who comes around." —Bruce Schindler

"I now have balance in life, feeling fulfilled, loved, appreciated, and have the ability to take care of family and still have enough to help others." —Steve Humble

"To be able to take care of my family and to be able to help others in need." —Bunny Lightsey

"My most important goal and accomplishment is the father that I have been to my four kids, and secondly, the friend that I have been to my close circle of friends." —Mickey Redwine

"It gave me more time to spend with my family and closest people that I love." —Jeb Lopez

Three Ways to Place a High Priority on Your Family Time

1. At the beginning of each week, schedule family time. Do not let anything get in the way of this precious time.

2. When you are together, let family members know that they have 100 percent of your attention. Refrain from checking work mail and texts, or taking telephone calls. If you feel compelled, update your message to read that you will be inaccessible for the evening or during the weekend due to scheduled family time. Your clients may be impressed!

3. Recognize that your actions will be a reflection of what your children will do to you when they are adults. Give them your uninterrupted time so that you can look forward to also receiving it from them when they are walking in your shoes as adults.

ACTION STEP: KEEP YOUR PRIORITIES IN CHECK BY REMEMBER-ING THE PEOPLE WHO ARE SUPPORTIVE OF YOU IN YOUR PER-SONAL LIFE.

They Are Philanthropists or They Pay It Forward

Secret 43 for Creating Your Own Success: Give Back

Giving back. When was the last time you did it?

Contrary to preconceived notions of the average Joe, most self-made millionaires are strong believers in giving back. In fact, I found that there is a definite impetus in these individuals for wanting to give back.

Why Do These People Give Back?

No matter how these individuals achieved their status, they give back for many reasons. Some give back because when they were in need, they remember that others were there for them. Others give back because they were once in need, yet had no one when they really needed the emotional and/or financial support. Yet others give back because they were on the road less traveled as they were working on "making it" and did not have precedent for how to achieve success. No matter the reason, these good

Samaritans give back because they thrive on making a difference in other people's lives.

When Did They Begin to Give Back?

Some were compelled to give back while they were working on achieving this success status. Others focused on giving back after achieving this milestone. Some did both. They gave back as they were becoming self-made millionaires and then increased their giving back after they made their first million.

How Do They Give Back?

Some of the self-made millionaires interviewed for this book give back in various ways. Some volunteer their time and expertise. Others become adjunct faculty members at their local college and/or university. One person gives back by mentoring women as well as ministering to the sick and helpless. Another gives back by donating his time at prisons to prepare individuals to begin their own enterprises when they are released. One of the thirty individuals interviewed gives back by donating to the arts in their community. Some provide financial support to others by donating to the organization of their choice.

Before you get in line for a handout from these individuals, recognize that there are no free lunches or free money to be had. These self-made millionaires are savvy givers to people and to organizations to which they can identify. They give back by giving individuals who want to succeed "the rod." They teach them how to fish rather than merely giving them the fish as you will read about in Secret 52 (You Have Been Given the Rod, Now Go Fish).

Although becoming a self-made millionaire was never a goal, Bill Dunn, the twenty-ninth self-made millionaire in this book, shared that one of his greatest satisfactions for achieving this status is being able to give large amounts of money to people and charities that never had the opportunities and support that he had over the years.

Personally, I love to give back. I love giving individuals the necessary tools to accomplish their defined goals. My way of giving back is by assisting people in believing in themselves, to give them the necessary confidence essential for creating their own success. My way of giving back is by writing this book—to assist you on your self-made millionaire journey.

Let me ask you the question once again: What are you presently doing to give back? Are you donating your time, your expertise, or monetary funds to others? Remember: You have to give it to get it. It is called the law of circulation.

You do not have to be a self-made millionaire to begin giving back. As you see, however, one of the fifty-two secrets for creating your own self-made millionaire status *is* by giving back. As Rodger DeRose, the thirteenth self-made millionaire interviewed for this book, advocates, "Leave a footprint in life. If you can't leave a footprint, leave a thumbprint."

Three Ways to Begin Giving Back

1. Write down your life accomplishments to date, both large and small. Evaluate how you achieved them.

2. Be accessible for individuals who can benefit from the steps you took to get you where you are today. Also, recognize that an appreciated form of giving back is simply lending an ear.

3. Recognize that it is essential to give what you get. If you want others to be accessible for you, give back to others who can benefit from what you learned in the school of hard knocks.

ACTION STEP: TAKE A PROACTIVE "GIVE BACK" APPROACH. BESIDES MAKING A DIFFERENCE IN ANOTHER PERSON'S LIFE, YOU WILL BE PLEASANTLY SURPRISED HOW GRATIFYING IT WILL BE.

They Are Good Stewards of Money

Secret 44 for Creating Your Own Success: Live Below Your Means

People choose to live one of three different ways: above their means, within their means, or below their means. Which one describes you?

If you live *above your means*, you make purchases using your credit cards that you may not be able to pay in full when your statements arrive. Living above your means may not afford you the extra cash for an emergency savings account or an investment account that will prepare you for your financial future.

If you live *within your means*, you make purchases using cash or your credit card. You pay your mortgage and other bills in full by the due date and have an emergency fund. You may have extra money to begin a savings account and investing for your financial future.

If you live *below your means*, you make extra monthly payments on your house mortgage, student loans, and other financial commitments. By living below your means, you also have an income available for an emergency fund and savings account. You have money left over to invest.

If you have not already guessed, self-made millionaires live below their means. They do not try to keep up with the Joneses. Instead, they begin with the end in mind: *financial freedom*. Only after assessing their financial responsibilities do they budget their surplus funds for expendable income as material things and entertainment. They choose financial freedom over buying that Ferrari on the corner lot.

Andy Hidalgo, the thirtieth self-made millionaire in this book, achieved this status at age forty-six. Andy knows the value of living below his means. He shared, "Living below your means is a characteristic developed in your youth and relates specifically to how you are either educated about money—if you are lucky— or how you see people work in relation to what they earn."

Some life lessons are best learned first-hand. Andy experienced the importance of "living below your means" as a child when his mom was unemployed and there were serious money problems. Even as a child he knew that, as an adult, he never wanted to be in a similar compromised economic position. He took preventive measures to avoid this from happening by learning how to become financially responsible.

Andy did this by managing what he made rather than creating the habit of spending what was earned. He also made a point of spending less for cautionary purposes such as unforeseen expenses.

For Andy, living below your means translated into buying only the things that would be enjoyed by his family or that were a necessity for him. As he and his wife were raising their four children, there were times that his family wanted something that may not have been a priority to Andy. A specific example was a beach house. His criteria for making this purchase was to first make sure that it was affordable in relation to his net worth.

Like many self-made millionaires, Andy's spending choices in life are to buy based on need and to save the rest for his family and their future generations. Living below his means has become a lifelong choice for Andy regarding how to manage money.

Four Advantages of Living Below Your Means

1. You will have more expendable income to pay off your debt faster.

2. You will be able to build your emergency savings.

3. You will be able to save a portion of your income to invest.

4. You will achieve financial freedom sooner.

ACTION STEP: ASSESS YOUR SPENDING HABITS. IF YOU DO NOT LIVE BELOW YOUR MEANS, FIGURE OUT THE UNNECESSARY EXPENSES THAT YOU CAN ELIMINATE.

Secret 45 for Creating Your Own Success: Create a Financial Road Map for Yourself

Most people interpret financial planning as an exercise to prepare for retirement. Financial planning, however, is an exercise essential for anyone and everyone and should begin the minute that first dollar touches an individual's hand.

Many people—me included—were not exposed to a money management course. Short of our parents' money-wise advice and proactively learning through online articles how to be financially savvy, many of us had to learn how to manage money through the school of hard knocks. In fact, it is easier for many people to make money than it is for them to manage it.

When beginning to write this section, I felt myself cringe at the thought of having to fill out a financial worksheet. I realized why I had despised this exercise for years. I felt boxed in and had a hunch what the end result would be: that I loved to spend money.

After reading *Financially SECURE Forever* by Charles Hamowy, I became aware of a new field of study called *neuroeconomics,* which is the study of how people make economic decisions.[1] It became much clearer about my own spending habits and factors that influenced my buying decisions. Like neuromarketers, I began to figure out why I buy the way I do. It also helped me to anticipate the challenges—in this case, my spending habits.

In order to create your financial road map, the first step is to become acquainted with how much you spend in relation to how much you earn. The end result will be for you to either congratulate yourself for spending less than you make or to shave off discretionary expenses. In either case, the ultimate goal will be for you to have 10 percent of your earnings left over to actually save and invest.

Sounds like a lot to chew. Stay with me. I can tell you firsthand that it is not as painful a process as it sounds.

Different Types of Budgets

Creating a budget for yourself is a personal decision. It should be one that works for you based on your personality and spending style.

If you are detail-oriented like my daughter, who is an amazing manager of her finances, you may create an Excel spreadsheet, list your expenses by category, and then log everything you buy. If that is too much information for you (as it is for me), you may prefer to create a general budget based on your essentials: your needs followed by your discretionary spending wants.

Then spend within your "need guidelines" by foregoing or delaying your wants.

A third type of budgeting is to figure out what is your cash flow and then to adapt your spending based on the amount you have available that month. No ifs, ands, or spending buts!

No matter what type of budget you choose, make sure that you select one that will work for you.

How to Use Budgeting Tools

Your budgeting tools can be as sophisticated as an Excel spreadsheet or a smartphone app such as Mint. You may prefer to keep budgeting simple by logging your available cash and expenses in a notebook.

Some people even use envelopes as their budgeting tools. They designate a certain amount of cash to put in each envelope for going out to eat and other leisure activities and then spend within their envelope means.

Budgeting does not have to be complicated. It is simply a means to hold yourself fiscally accountable.

It goes without saying that your first goal is to *earn more than you spend.* If you find that you have been doing the reverse— spending more than you make—mapping out your current spending habits is a great beginning. In fact, you are welcome to join me in making Dru Riess, the twenty-second self-made millionaire interviewed for this book, your guru.

After Dru achieved self-made millionaire status in his late twenties, he and his spouse did not go wild like many who achieved millionaire status and then lost it by overspending.

Instead, Dru and his spouse made a choice to live way below their means.

Here's how Dru explained it:

I was a millionaire in my late twenties if you look at my personal balance sheet, but at thirty I had millions in liquid cash in my personal bank accounts in addition to the assets on my personal balance sheet. I took all the money and put it in a "vault." I don't look at it and I do not touch it. I put it with a financial firm and told them in twenty-five years (when I am fifty-five), I will come for it. By that time it will be so much money my kids can't run out of it. Until then my wife and I both work and we are living our life paycheck to paycheck. Big paychecks though!

I don't know about you, however I am sufficiently impressed.

Four Financial Planning Strategies

1. **Analyze your budget.** See where you have room for improvement. If your completed worksheet shows that you are spending more than you make, reevaluate your spending style. As you do, recognize your relationship with money. What percentage of your spending is based on needs versus wants? Take the necessary steps to shave off your "spending wants."

2. **Make a point of spending with intention.** As shared in Secret 47 (Preplan Your Purchases), this action alone will help you to avoid making impulsive purchases and instead map out your purchases.

3. **Create a short-term and long-term financial plan.**

   › *Short-term:* Perhaps you want to save for a down payment for a house or condo. Or you want to set enough money aside so that when you need (not want) a new car, you can pay for it in cash.

> ▸ ***Long-term:*** Your intention is to retire in X (number of) years. Figure out the lifestyle that you see yourself enjoying and the annual amount that you will need to live. Then based on the amount that you will commit to saving and investing between now and the number of years, see if what you will be saving from this day forward will be sufficient to live your intended lifestyle. There are numerous retirement calculators available for you online.

4. **Invest for your future.** Besides doing a great job planning for his financial future, John Pierce, the fourteenth self-made millionaire in this book, has spent more than twenty-five years in the investment arena. This self-made millionaire recommends that individuals set up a 401(k) and contribute 10 percent to it annually. John went on to explain how this pretax contribution has a minimal effect on your take-home pay. He ensures that anyone who contributes 10 percent to a 401(k) beginning in their twenties will retire a millionaire.

John also advises a simple 70/30 stock to bond mix using re-balanced exchange-traded funds through the advice of a human being rather than an algorithm and later more conservative asset allocation. John also shared that if individuals do not have a 401(k), they should contribute to an IRA.

John shared that he started investing the day he got a job. He explained that he started at a 10-percent contribution rate in all equities. He then continued to max out (usually increases each year at $18,000 per year). This savvy investor recommends creating investments in all equities. The reason is if you are investing for thirty to forty years, it doesn't matter: You will earn 5 to 8 percent and retire a millionaire.

John's last piece of advice for investing in your future is to google "The Rule of Seven" to understand the power of compounding. The premise is that your money invested will double every seven years and with that magic (no magic—just math) you become a millionaire.

As you continue to read this book, you will see from the comments by the self-made millionaires that it really isn't about the money. Let's face it, however: As money gave these thirty self-made individuals financial freedom, mapping out and living within the boundaries of your financial road map will also give you financial power and much less stress.

Control what you spend rather than having expenses control you. Above all, recognize that "money is your friend" if you treat it with respect.

ACTION STEP: TAKE CONTROL OF YOUR FUTURE BY CREATING YOUR FINANCIAL ROAD MAP.

They Are in Control of Their Financial Destiny

Secret 46 for Creating Your Own Success: Pay Yourself First

Have you heard the "sagely" advice to pay yourself first?

If you are like most Americans, you have not followed this counsel. In fact, 26 percent of Americans do not even have an emergency savings account let alone are following the practice of "paying yourself first."[1]

You may be wondering how you can even think about paying yourself first when you haven't built a savings account for those unexpected expenses.

Let me suggest a few ways to begin by working on both building an emergency fund *and* paying yourself first.

How to Build an Emergency Fund

Start by evaluating your existing fixed expenses. Review your current cell phone data usage to see what you can save monthly by lowering what you are not using. Ask your car insurance provider what your savings will be by increasing your deductible. If you have credit card debt, talk with your banker to apply for a consolidation loan. Besides feeling less overwhelmed by receiving only one credit card bill a month, you may also be able to pay a lower interest rate, which will allow you to pay off your debt faster.

Review what you spend on monthly expenses "of your choice." That includes eating out, entertainment, and gifts. Curb your spending by packing your lunch, eating at home more often, and buying birthday gifts when you see them rather than waiting until the last minute and paying more.

Reevaluate where you live. If you presently rent a two-bedroom apartment with a view, consider moving to a one-bedroom apartment without a view. Your savings will be substantial, allowing you to build your emergency fund quicker and begin paying yourself first that much sooner.

If you have a car payment, consider selling your car and buying one with the cash that you get for your car. Though you may have to swallow your pride, you will smile when you see that you can build your emergency fund with that extra $200 to $400 a month rather than spending it on something that depreciates, like a car.

When you get a raise, have the increase go directly into your emergency fund. Whether you are able to shave off $30 or $500 from your fixed and discretionary monthly expenses, take whatever you are able to save no matter the amount.

Set a goal to have three to six months of living expenses saved by a given time. It may take a while to save six months of living expenses, but worry not: You are moving in the right direction by having created a master plan.

Start "Paying Yourself First"

Rather than waiting until you have your emergency fund built, begin planning for your financial future with your next paycheck. The easiest way to do this is to arrange with your payroll service to have a certain percentage of your net income go directly into an interest-bearing savings account.

Most financial planners recommend that you pay yourself 10 percent of your net income. For instance, let's say that your monthly net income is $2,400 and you get paid twice a month. Request that your payroll service deposits $120 per paycheck (or $240 monthly) into your "pay it first" account. Just think: In one year, you will have saved $2,880. If you invest that amount annually— not including any raises that you will receive—you will be building a nest egg to achieve financial freedom.

You also will feel in control of your life by having mapped out your financial future.

ACTION STEP: START PAYING YOURSELF NOW.

Secret 47 for Creating Your Own Success: Preplan Your Purchases

If I had to select one secret in this book that many people have not learned to do, it would be preplanning purchases. Shopping is therapy for many, which contributes to impulsive buying. And I have been one of them!

If you read the Introduction, then you noticed I am not *yet* a self-made millionaire. I have five secrets to go, and Secret 47 is definitely one of them.

Thinking before making small purchases was not high on my list. For that reason alone, preplanning my purchases has become a new habit that I diligently integrated into my way of life when I began writing this book in summer 2017. I must admit that now, before visiting my favorite online shopping sites, I remind myself that I am merely "browsing." I also have stopped watching infomercials recognizing that I am perfect bait for those slick sales pitches.

Now, when going to the mall, I walk in armed with a list of exactly what I *need* to buy. If there is something that I want, I put it on the list for the next visit in order to plan ahead and condition myself to *make preplanned purchases.*

Positive results are terrific incentives. Just listen to this: The first month that I made a point of preplanning my purchases, my credit card bill was cut by 25 percent. (I am talking about $40 here, and about $50 dollars there, which I did not realize added up!) That was enough incentive for me to stay on course. I took the money that I would have spent on unplanned purchases and transferred it from my checking account to a special savings account.

Why didn't someone pound this success secret into my brain decades ago? Perhaps they did and I did not listen. Oops! Another self-made secret yet to be mastered!

Can you relate? If impulse buying has been secretly undermining you from keeping your hard-earned money, read on.

Five Ways to Beat Your Spending Urge

1. **Don't leave home or go online without a list.** It's all about the list. By mapping out what you need versus want to buy, you will be much more time and cost efficient.

2. **After making your list, check it twice.** Double-check to make sure that you really need what is on your list. How often have you bought toothpaste, that box of rice

pilaf, or facial cream only to realize that you already had what you needed in the back of your cupboard? If you are guilty of buying things you already have, reread Secret 15 for Creating Your Own Success (Become a Minimalist).

3. **Monitor what you saved.** At the end of each month, compare what you saved within the past three months. Then put that extra money to good use by creating a special savings account. You will be surprised how much surplus cash you will have over a period of a year.

4. **Reward yourself for resisting the urge to spend.** At the end of each month, calculate what you saved by holding yourself accountable with a list. If you are having withdrawal symptoms from your shopping sprees, reward yourself with a gift card in the amount of 10 to 20 percent of what you saved. By putting this behavior-modification strategy into practice, you will have the best of both worlds. You also will be more likely to make your new "preplan your purchase system" a regular part of your lifestyle.

5. **Recognize that you may enjoy the spending chase more than the catch.** By mastering your impulsive urge to spend, you also may realize that buying things was not about needing them in the first place. Making unplanned purchases may have been a form of therapy for you. Just think about how stress free you will be with smaller bills at the end of each month.

ACTION STEP: IF IT IS NOT ON THE LIST, RESIST THE URGE TO BUY IT.

They Build Their Wealth

Secret 48 for Creating Your Own Success: Create Multiple Sources of Income

One of the biggest differences between the masses and self-made millionaires or those in-the-making is the number of income streams they have.

Self-made millionaires create multiple sources of income one step at a time. Because there are only so many hours in the day, even today most successful individuals have one source of *active* income and at least two sources of *passive* income.

What most people do not realize, however, is that these individuals did something vastly different from the majority of Americans. They worked hard to create multiple sources of income, and so can you!

More than half of all U.S. families own stock, from workers who got automatically enrolled in their 401(k) retirement accounts to day traders working their personal accounts.[1] Study after study has shown that the best passive income for building wealth is to invest in dividend-paying stocks. Consider these other sources:

> ➤ Employer-matched contributions is free money.

> ➤ Creating a second source of income simply requires a convincing nature, sweat equity, and little, if any up-front cash.

> ➤ Everyone has a book inside of them and print-on-demand publishing houses are rampant.

A July 14, 2017 article on investing on bankrate.com cites the IRS findings that passive income typically comes from two sources: rental income or a business in which the person benefitting from the income no longer participates. Two specific examples mentioned are book royalties and dividend paying stocks.[2]

If you are reading this book, I implore you to take Secret 48 seriously. Putting into motion what it will take to create multiple streams of income that will work for you over time and provide you with financial freedom will change your life.

For the first thirty-five years of my life, I had only one source of income. The second, third, fourth, and fifth sources of income were created initially as marketing tools for my consulting business that I had started (Secret 37: Reinvent Yourself) on a shoe-string budget.

Although I did not have marketing dollars, I did have chutz-pah (pretty good for being of Lebanese and Syrian descent). I envisioned (Secret 5: Visualize) a "Business Manners" column in city-wide newspapers.

Believe me: It didn't just happen. I followed up and followed through with a Gannet newspaper for nine months nearly begging them (Secret 33: Ask Until You Get a Yes) to pick up my column.

After finally getting a yes, I decided to contact twenty other newspapers. Over a two-year period (Secret 21: Persevere), three other publications picked up the column. Although paid a pittance, I was thrilled to have found a way to generate three additional sources of income by writing one column and having it appear in four weekly papers.

The weekly columns were generating local business in the cities in which they were circulated. I decided, however, that I wanted national exposure (Secret 36: The Sky Is the Limit). I researched the business magazines that had an international audience. Starting with a telephone call (that was the way to do it in the 1990s), I followed up by sending a cover letter and three sample columns formatted for their publication. Another follow-up call or two. After thirty rejections, a national magazine picked up my column. This income stream provided my firm with international exposure, which introduced me to the life of a road warrior.

Besides being instrumental in helping my business to thrive, these newspaper and magazine columns opened doors for additional sources of income. Two years prior, I had visualized writing a book and, yes, had made it one of my documented goals (Secret 6: Set Meaningful Goals). I did not recognize it, however, when it fell in my lap. Scott Adams, the then-publisher/owner of Adams Media, had read a newspaper article about our firm in *USA Today* and called to ask if I would submit a book proposal.

One more income stream! A book advance with royalties to follow meant an additional stream of income. Little did I know that my first book would lead to writing eight more books over a twenty-five-year period.

Income streams do more than generate cash. They create opportunities to diverse income sources. My income streams afforded me to personally buy a building and a second home out of state.

Despite these sources of revenue, there was something wrong with this picture. I was still working hard rather than smart. At the age of forty-two, I was ignorant to the most important way to plan for my financial future: a retirement account. Luckily, I finally set up a retirement account and maxed out the annual amount that could be funded.

Like many people, however, I was afraid to build my wealth by investing in the stock market. I was fearful of losing my hard-earned money. So against my accountant and investment advisor's advice, I put my money exclusively in certificates of deposit for more than twenty years, though I logically knew that these CDs were not even keeping up with the cost of inflation. My financial ignorance and fear of losing what I had saved ruled.

Finally, five years ago I saw the light and began investing in the stock market. My portfolio balance is proof of how the power of compounding creates wealth.

The reason I am sharing my vulnerability with you is for you to learn from what I did wrong. I hope you will see how you can easily build multiple streams of income by starting a business and freelancing with a lot of sweat equity and little cash up-front. I also hope that you see how the right real estate investment(s) can become a great stream of income.

I hope you will learn from my ignorance and begin having deducted as much as you can afford from your next paycheck and those that follow. Finally, I hope that you will begin investing your money wisely in dividend-paying growth stocks to allow your hard-earned money to multiply for you.

Eight Ideas for Putting Cash in Your Pocket

1. If you are having a hard time generating income streams, think about small ways to begin for putting cash in your pocket to invest. Take Sam Walton, the Walmart Founder's advice by "thinking big and acting small."[3]

2. Start looking for low-hanging fruit. For example, if your company has a 401(k) match, make sure you are contributing to get at least their maximum match.

3. Maximize cash back and other opportunities to put savings in your pocket. Most companies have partnerships with others. For instance, my cell phone service provider pays for my annual AAA membership.

4. Take advantage of cash back sites for online purchases. Visit sites like *www.topcashback.com* before making your regular purchases to receive a percentage back.

5. List your home with Airbnb.

6. Assess your material contents and sell what you no longer want or need.

7. Sign up as a driver with Uber, Lyft, Sidecar, or other car ride services in your area.

8. Earn your real estate license and align yourself with seasoned realtors to do weekend open houses for them.

ACTION STEP: GET STARTED!

They Monetize Their Expertise

Secret 49 for Creating Your Own Success: Start a Business

Thomas Edison did it. Andrew Carnegie did it. Mark Zuckerberg did it and so did Jeff Bezos. These entrepreneurs all started their businesses from the ground up.

- According to investfourmore.com, 75 percent of millionaires are self-employed—even though only 20 percent of the workforce is self-employed.[1]

- Seventy-six percent of the thirty self-made millionaires who were randomly chosen to be part of this book started their own businesses.

- Six percent of the individuals acquired an already established business.

- Thirteen percent worked in high-level managerial/partner positions in the professional services industry.

> One percent of the individuals interviewed for this book was in the arts.

> The 90 percent (twenty-seven individuals) who built businesses from the ground up did so based on one of the three following ways:

1. They saw a need for a product or service.

2. They built their business around a marketable skill that they possessed.

3. They had a passion that they wanted to share with the world.

Let me give you some examples of businesses started by the self-made millionaires in this book.

Identify a Need

Dr. Zachary Berk, OD, HappCo's founder, began this business as a result of recognizing that happy employees are more productive team members. HappCo's service includes a mindfulness program, which increases employees' focus, collaboration, compassion, happiness, and engagement. This serial entrepreneur started more than twenty healthcare companies during the past three decades.

Monetize an Existing Skill

Jason Phillips is described by CNBC as the "King of Color." Although it took him more than a decade to determine the best business model to begin his own painting and home repair company, in 1997 Jason started Phillips Home Improvement. In 2017, Jason and his fifty-three employees generated $11 million.

Sarian Bouma began a commercial cleaning service and built a staff of two hundred employees. Her decision to start Capitol Hill Building Maintenance in 1987 was as a result of the accolades she had received from customers during her freelance cleaning jobs.

Turn a Passion Into a Business

Bruce Schindler had carving in his genes. His grandfather loved carving silver and wood. His father, a German hard-core perfectionist, was a cabinet maker. Between his DNA and his move to Skagway, Alaska, Bruce became fascinated with 35,000-year-old mammoths. As a result, Bruce developed a passion for carving fossilized ivory and began Schindler Carvings in 1995.

Though it is exciting to begin a business, recognize that a strong work ethic and positive attitude, along with the other forty-nine secrets described in this book, are essential for growing your own small business. If you are up for the challenge, go for it!

Five Steps for Beginning a Business

1. **Do your homework.** Explore companies around the country that are providing the service or product that you are considering. Ask the owners of those enterprises if you could work alongside them gratis as a way of learning what it will take to launch your enterprise. (See Secret 27: Surround Yourself With People You Want to Be Like.)

2. **Meet with an accountant, attorney, and web designer who specialize in small businesses.** Your accountant will help you decide if you should set up your business as a partnership, an LLC, or an S or C Corporation. This individual will file the necessary paperwork and also apply for an Employer Identification Number (EIN), which is equivalent to a social security number for your business. Your attorney will file the necessary paperwork for your business name, license, if necessary, and any other legal

forms to operate. These individuals will be essential in laying the groundwork for establishing the framework for your business.

3. **Be realistic in recognizing that you have to spend it to make it.** Recognize that there will be up-front costs for starting a business. If you do not have capital set aside to fund your business, consider beginning it part time during evenings and weekends while you are working your full-time job. Whatever you do, minimize the amount of debt you incur.

4. **Hire independent contractors.** When first beginning your business, hire independent contractors on an "as-needed" basis. As your business grows, hire part-time employees. When your business revenues justify it, hire full-time employees. These hiring measures will assist you in minimizing your overhead, an essential factor for keeping your debt low.

5. **Follow the "just in time" buying approach.** Keep your inventory to a minimum. Invest in the necessary products and services as orders are received. Successful corporations follow this practice. So should you.

ACTION STEP: RESEARCH AND PREPLAN YOUR BUSINESS PRIOR TO LAUNCHING IT.

They Think Long-Term

Secret 50 for Creating Your Own Success: Delay Short-Term Gratification

Essential attributes that differentiates the person who lives for today from self-made millionaires are their buying habits, the manner in which they satisfy their wants and needs, and the way they live their everyday lives in order to plan for their future wants and needs.

Individuals who thrive on instant gratification often base their purchasing decisions on their *emotional wants*. Those who delay instant gratification are big-picture thinkers and make purchasing decisions based on their *needs*. They delay their emotional wants in order to accomplish their long-term goals faster.

Unfortunately, most people have not been taught this skill. Those who have been exposed to this secret may not have listened if they were told about the importance of delaying their short-term wants by placing more attention on their immediate needs. Figure out which one describes you.

If you are a short-term thinker, you spend a large percentage of your take-home pay on your *wants* versus your *needs*. That may include spending more than 90 percent of your income on:

> ➤ Payment for the car that you have always wanted.

> ➤ Rent in an apartment building where you have always wanted to live.

> ➤ Eating out and ordering in several times a week.

> ➤ Working out at the most exclusive gym rather than at the local rec center.

> ➤ Going on a quarterly getaway to de-stress.

> ➤ Shopping on your favorite website as a form of therapy for that new outfit that will get you out of your funk.

Sounds great, doesn't it? It definitely is, at least for the short term.

On the opposite end of the spectrum, if you are a person who delays instant gratification by looking at the big picture, the following situations better describe you:

> ➤ You would have liked that new sports car, but instead gladly accepted the one that your grandpa had been driving for ten years before turning it over to you.

> ➤ You would rather have had your own place to live after graduation, but you moved back home with your parents in order to save money for a down payment for your first house or condo.

> ➤ You decided to share an apartment with three other people in order to save 75 percent of the rent that you would have spent for the newly built apartments in the city.

> ▸ You plan one vacation a year rather than succumbing to the impulsive getaways planned by your friends.

> ▸ You balance packing your lunch a few days a week with going out to eat with your work colleagues the other two days to remain sociable.

> ▸ You make dinner at home more often than going out to eat or using Grubhub to order in regularly.

> ▸ You go "shopping" in your closet to mix and match what you already own when you feel like wearing something new.

If you are the first type of person, you are living in the now. If, however, the second set of actions describes you, you delay short-term gratification for the long-term benefit. Guess what? You are in control of both your life and your finances!

In fact, you have one of the most important secrets for success: *You delay short-term gratification!* Whether you know it or not, you have laid the groundwork for becoming a self-made millionaire.

This need to teach the impact of between living in the now or living to build your future became very clear to me to three years ago when I was presenting a "polish for building profits" training program. It was for a group of individuals who had been in their careers for one year. They were selected for the training because they were considered leaders-in-the-making by their managers.

Within the first thirty minutes of the training, however, I realized that these budding individuals needed more than professional grooming for climbing their organization's slippery ladder of success. They also needed a few vital tips for achieving their *own* personal success.

Let me give you the specific scenario:

I asked participants what personal goals they had accomplished since they started working full-time. One individual said that he bought a new car. Another new hire said that she was living in a part of the city where she always dreamed of being.

The third individual—who appeared to be the most quiet and rather nerdy person in the room—raised his hand and said, "I make a point of saving $1,000 a month from my paycheck."

When asked how he did it with a starting salary commensurate with his other colleagues in the room, he said:

> My goal is to become a millionaire. I once read that in order to do that, I have to delay my immediate wants for my future ones. So while I am often tempted to do otherwise, I go to lunch with friends once a week and pack sandwiches the other four days. I make coffee at home rather than buying it. I volunteer my time at a dog shelter as my extracurricular activity. I have a basic work wardrobe and plan what I need and then ask for the items for birthday and holiday gifts.

Talk about impressive! He sounded to me like he was on the road to becoming a self-made millionaire.

He was a visionary. His intention was to become a millionaire. He had a documented goal of saving $1,000 a month (this is not a typo: $1,000 a month!) and he was putting it into practice.

He set aside his immediate needs to focus on a long-term goal by packing lunch and making coffee rather than stopping on the way to work to buy that $5 cup of coffee.

Whether he realized it or not, he was even paying it forward by volunteering at a dog shelter.

The other individuals in the room—his manager included—were awed by his comments. So was I! In fact, his words acted as the clincher to motivate me to write this book.

In addition to being groomed for professional success, I realized that our future business leaders, our Millennial generation, also deserve to be given the secrets for achieving personal success. In other words, they should be taught how they can have anything they want in their personal lives by learning what self-made millionaires do that most people don't.

So you see that short-term gratification serves your immediate emotional needs. When you take a step back, however, to see where a short-term decision is going to take you in the long run, you may think twice about it.

Avoid succumbing to instant gratification and short-term thinking. Instead, make it a habit to work toward your long-term goals.

Self-made millionaires think long-term. They define what they want to accomplish by looking at the big picture.

Three Ways to Delay Short-Term Gratification

1. Assess your present buying habits. Write down the last three purchases you made. Were they based on meeting your instant gratification wants or your specific needs?

2. Figure out the value that your past three instant gratification purchases have in your present life. Do they add value to your life or were they a form of instant therapy to relieve your work overload stress?

3. Commit to delaying future short-term gratification. Think before you commit to a purchase. Ask yourself if the purchase will take you one step closer to achieving your long-term personal goals.

ACTION STEP: AS YOU MAKE PURCHASES, ASSESS THE VALUE THAT THEY WILL HAVE FOR ACCOMPLISHING YOUR LONG-TERM GOALS.

Habit 25

They Enjoy the Journey as Much as the Destination

Secret 51 for Creating Your Own Success: Recognize That It Is Not About the Money

My godfather, Uncle Phil, owned a small corner grocery store from the 1940s through the 1960s. Credit cards did not exist in the 1940s, so when his customers bought groceries, they paid Uncle Phil in cash.

Rather than depositing money in the bank, my mom told me that Uncle Phil kept his money in safety deposit boxes—in his home, that is. He would stash money in coffee cans under the kitchen sink, in the freezer, under the mattress, in the attic, virtually everywhere you could imagine. A thief's haven—if only they had known!

Although I was only twelve, I will never forget the Thanksgiving dinner that my Uncle Phil shared with us. We were sitting around the dining room table having dessert as my parents and Uncle Phil were reminiscing about "the good ol' days."

We all knew that his days were numbered. Uncle Phil had been diagnosed with terminal cancer months earlier.

My mom asked, "Phil, if you could live your life over again, what would you have done differently?" I will never forget my Uncle Phil's words: "I forgot to have fun."

Let's face it: Money buys a life of ease and luxury. Money certainly provides the opportunities to live life to its fullest. Is that, however, enough?

As you will see in the following comments, there are certain things that money can't buy. From the mouths of nine of the self-made millionaires in this book:

"Don't put too much weight in your financial success. No amount of money is worth sacrificing the health and happiness of your family, friends, and ultimately yourself." —Bruce Schindler

"Don't worry about the 'millionaire' part. If you drop that thought from your mind and just focus on creating and doing, you will get there faster. Anything you do should never be about the money, or you will either fail or ultimately not be happy." —Brian Wong

"Don't think about the money, happiness is the most important thing. Find a profession that encourages growth while providing intellectual stimulation. That way if you don't make money you still will feel a sense of achievement and success. Lots of unhappy millionaires out there." —Bill Dunn

"Don't focus on the millions or the number. Focus on how you can add value using your specific gifts and strengths. That's the key." —Shama Hyder

"Don't focus on the money. Focus on doing an incredible job and enjoying your life while you do it." —Steve Humble

"Don't focus on the money. Do what you love. When you do make it, don't try to hold on to all of it for yourself. Take care of those that need to be taken care of." —Bunny Lightsey

"Be patient with yourself. Rome wasn't built in a day, and your success won't be achieved overnight either. Take your time. Make sure that you have a solid spiritual life, and take time to attend to your spiritual and emotional life. They are more important than you think. Try to be a good person." —Gary M.

"Money doesn't buy love, or happiness, it only complicates things in the long run." —Joe Palko

"Never make money be the sole source of motivation." —John M.

ACTION STEP: WRITE DOWN WHAT YOU CURRENTLY HAVE THAT MONEY CANNOT BUY. ALSO, WRITE DOWN WHAT YOU WOULD LIKE TO HAVE THAT MONEY THAT CANNOT BUY.

Secret 52 for Creating Your Own Success: You Have Been Given the Rod, Now Go Fish

If you have gotten to this page, then there is a good chance that you have finished reading *What Self-Made Millionaires Do That Most People Don't: 52 Ways to Create Your Own Success.*

You have been given the secrets for becoming a self-made millionaire. Now it is your turn to put them into practice. Get started with this five-step approach.

The Five-Step Approach for Achieving Your Self-Made Millionaire Status

1. Go to page 219 and write down each of the fifty-two secrets that you have already accomplished for creating your own success. For instance, if you have a regular exercise routine, then give yourself credit by writing down Secret 25 for Creating Your Own Success: Exercise for the Health of It. Or, if you are relentless when you begin a project and figure what you need to do to see it through to completion, then also give yourself credit for Secret 21 for Creating Your Own Success: Persevere.

2. Now, write down the secrets that you have yet to master on page 221. For example, if one of the secrets that you have yet to accomplish is Secret 10 for Creating Your Own Success: Be a Time Master and you know it because you are often late, then write that secret on your "to be mastered" list. Or, if you make unplanned purchases when you go shopping, then write down Secret 47 for Creating Your Own Success: Preplan Your Purchases.

3. Next, prioritize the secrets that you will work on making part of your daily style. Work on mastering one success secret at a time and enjoy the process.

4. Next to each one, write down what you will do differently from what you are presently doing. For instance, if you run late, write "I will write down the time that I have to leave rather than the time that I have to be somewhere." If you are an impulsive buyer when you go to the grocery store, surf your favorite online buying site or go to the mall, then commit to yourself by writing "I will buy only what is on my list."

5. Catch yourself doing it right. Each time you catch yourself modifying a behavior, congratulate yourself by acknowledging it in writing. For example, if you are working on Secret 10 for Creating Your Own Success: Be a Time Master and you get to the destination by the given time (or earlier), give yourself credit by writing "By writing down the time I had to leave rather than the time I had to be at my destination, I am learning how to be a master of my time."

ACTION STEP: DESIGNATE A START DATE WHEN YOU WILL *BEGIN* INTEGRATING THE SECRETS YOU HAVE YET TO MASTER INTO YOUR LIFE. GIVE A REALISTIC *END DATE* WHEN YOU ARE CONFIDENT THAT THE SECRETS YOU HAVE YET TO MASTER WILL BECOME A REGULAR PART OF YOUR LIFESTYLE.

Afterword

Thank you for taking time from your busy schedule to finish this book. I hope that it has inspired you to elevate your expectations regarding what you can accomplish.

I look forward to hearing the impact that this book has had in assisting you in achieving self-made millionaire status. Please remember that, as Confucius says, "A thousand mile journey begins with one step." Because I am sure that you have already mastered several of the fifty-two secrets, you can see an end in sight.

Writing this book has been a real exercise for me. Though it was meant for you, the reader, to discover the fifty-two secrets for creating your own success, I must tell you that it has also moved me closer to the self-made millionaire finish line.

As I wrote each section, I kept track of the secrets that were part of my existing way of being. I also took a second look at the five secrets that I have yet to master. They are:

➤ **Secret 14: Learn Something New Every Day.** Now I make a point of listening to a TED Talk or other podcast when I am on the treadmill or driving.

➤ **Secret 25: Exercise for the Health of It.** I have committed to exercising on my own and/or with a trainer thirty minutes a day for five days a week.

➤ **Secret 41: Be Grateful.** I bought a gratitude journal and each evening before going to bed write down the things that happened each day for which I am thankful.

➤ **Secret 46: Pay Yourself First.** I linked a savings account to my payroll service to have 10 percent automatically go into that account.

➤ **Secret 47: Preplan Your Purchases.** I have made a point of making a list before going shopping online or to a store and have not deviated by buying what has not been on the list.

I have projected a specific date for getting to the self-made millionaire finish line: January 30, 2020. That gives me nineteen months to making these secrets a regular part of my life.

What about you? Please let me know the secrets that you have yet to master along with the deadline you have given yourself to get the self-made millionaire finish line.

I welcome you to email me along the way. I will be happy to answer any specific questions that you have as you continue on your journey. I will be happy to send them to the self-made millionaires in this book who may guide you along the way.

Remember to enjoy the journey as much as the destination.

Ann Marie Sabath

www.annmariesabath.com

Appendix

List of Contributors

Jim Abraham

This very quiet man who was born into a Syrian immigrant family became a real estate mogul in his sixties. His first job was sweeping floors and selling popcorn before working inside Mischka's Candy Store and Café, which he eventually bought.

The "two cents, two cents, two cents" mantra that Jim would mutter each time he dipped caramel turtles into chocolate added up. For more than three decades, he bought parcels of land in Amherst, Ohio, and surrounding areas with the money that he generated from making and selling candy. His purchased land eventually became prime pieces of commercial property. Jim Abraham's story is told through his daughter in Secret 37 (Reinvent Yourself).

Zachary Berk

Dr. Zachary Berk, OD, is the Chief Happiness Officer of HappCo (*www.happco.com*), an innovative New York–based software company that combines technology, data, and service to help organizations know if their employees are happy and engaged. Zach became a self-made millionaire at age forty-five. This serial entrepreneur has been instrumental in starting more than twenty-five companies.

He is quoted in Secret 2 (Define What Success Means to You), in Secret 30 (Be Happy), in Secret 49 (Start A Business), and in First-Hand Advice to Readers Who Are Ready To Begin Their Self-Made Millionaire Journey.

Sarian Bouma

Sarian is the author of *Welfare to Millionaire: Heart of a Winner.* She became a self-made millionaire in her mid-thirties. Pretty good for someone who came to the United States from Sierra Leone, Africa, at nineteen only to find herself on welfare five years later. Sarian's tenacity gave her the strength to take control of her life when she realized she did not have enough food stamps to buy milk for her baby.

Sarian's inner strength and faith helped her to pick herself up, brush herself off, and get trained to go into the workforce. After working as a maid, Sarian was trained to become a bank teller and credit union manager. In 1987, Sarian founded Capitol Hill Building Maintenance Inc. headquartered in Lexington Park, Maryland. During a twenty-year period, she employed more than two hundred individuals. Besides training them for their jobs, she taught them to hold their heads up high. Sarian's story is part of Secret 7 (Take Control of Your Life) She is also mentioned in Secret 10 (Be A Time Master), Secret 32 (Challenge Yourself), and in Secret 49 (Start a Business).

Thomas Corley

Tom is a CPA, CFP, and holds a master's degree in taxation. He achieved self-made millionaire status at age fifty-four. Tom attributes much of his success to dream-setting—creating a blueprint of your ideal, future life and then pursuing specific dreams and the goals behind those dreams. He is mentioned in Secret 2 (Define What Success Means to You, Secret 5 (Visualize), Secret 13 (Be A Life-Long Learner), and Secret 20 (Turn Failures Into Opportunities).

Tom has written four books on rich habits. His most recent book, *Rich Habits, Poor Habits,* was released in October 2017.

Chuck Ceccarelli

Chuck is the owner and director of excitement of In the Ditch Towing Products (*www.intheditch.com*), based in Mountain Home, Idaho, and Rimco Inc. This entrepreneur is also the inventor of the SidePuller™. His success is based on two things: a strong work ethic and being determined. His $24-million-a-year business employs eighty full-time employees. Although Chuck had no formal education, he continues to learn from the best. Chuck surrounds himself with mentors and puts into practice the advice that works best for him and his organization. He became a millionaire in his late forties and is quoted in First-Hand Advice to Readers Who Are Ready to Begin Their Self-Made Millionaire Journey and in Secret 28 (Become a Brain-Trust Advisor).

Rodger DeRose

Rodger is the president and CEO of the Kessler Foundation (*www.kesslerfoundation.org*), one of the largest public charities in the United States supporting people with disabilities. An important part of Rodger's life is being physically fit. He is mentioned in Secret 2 (Define What Success Means to You), Secret 25 (Exercise for the Health of It, Secret 43 (Give Back), and in First-Hand Advice to Readers Who Are Ready to Begin Their Self-Made Millionaire Journey. Rodger became a self-made millionaire in his mid-forties.

Bill Dunn

Based in Charleston, South Carolina, Bill spent the past three decades at PricewaterhouseCoopers. He became a self-made millionaire in his mid-thirties, which afforded him the ability to do things that made him happy without fear of monetary or other stress. Bill places a high value on philanthropy. He is mentioned in Secret 2 (Define What Success Means to You), Secret 43 (Give Back), and Secret 51 (Recognize That It Is Not About the Money).

Laura FitzGerald

Laura plays a "man's game" for a living as a "land and mineral rights person" (*www.iliosresources.com*). Laura finds, buys, sells, brokers, and leases land for mineral rights (oil and gas). Since 2004, Laura has accumulated more than 40,000 acres of mineral rights, which has made her millions. Laura is often quoted as saying "I've made others millions of dollars. I can make you millions too." Laura is featured in Secret 4 (Believe in Yourself).

Andy Hidalgo

Andy is the chairman and CEO of H/Cell Energy Corporation (OTCQB:HCCC; *www.hcellenergy.com*), headquartered in Flemington, New Jersey. H/Cell Energy Corporation is a clean energy company serving commercial and government sectors worldwide. Andy became a self-made millionaire at age forty-six as a result of living frugally. He is quoted in Secret 1 (Create a Millionaire Mindset), Secret 2 (Define What Success Means to You), Secret 20 (Turn Failures Into Opportunities), and Secret 44 (Live Below Your Means).

Steve Humble

Steve founded Creative Home Engineering (*www.hiddenpassageway.com*) in 2004. This one-of-a-kind engineering firm specializes in the design and fabrication of ultra-secret motorized hidden passageways and vault doors in elite homes both domestically and internationally. Steve became a self-made millionaire at age thirty-eight. He attributes overcoming obstacles while growing his business to maintaining a positive attitude. He is quoted in Secret 2 (Define What Success Means to You), Secret 29 (Stay Positive), Secret 42 (Place a High Value on Your Personal Live), Secret 44 (Live Below Your Means), and Secret 51 (Recognize That It Is Not About the Money).

Shama Hyder

Shama started and ran a million-dollar company by age twenty-seven. Born in India, Shama came to the United States at age nine. She learned that sheer determination allowed her to thrive in a foreign environment.

Shama (*www.shamahyder.com*) founded The Marketing Zen Group, a global online marketing and digital PR company. She has been dubbed the "Zen Master of Marketing" by *Entrepreneur* magazine and the "Millennial Master of the Universe" by FastCompany.com. Shama has also been recognized as one of the top one hundred young entrepreneurs in the country and has been honored at both the White House and the United Nations. Her pearls of wisdom are featured in Secret 36 (The Sky Is the Limit) and Secret 51 (It Is Not About the Money).

Laura Kozlowski

Thanks to Laura Kozlowski's power to delegate to her very competent assistants, she became a top-producing loan officer for one of the nation's largest mortgage companies. She made her first million in that role when she was in her forties. Laura attributes her success to using her time wisely by focusing her energy working *on* business rather than *in* business. She is quoted in Secret 18 and in the First-Hand Advice to Readers Who Are Ready to Begin Their Self-Made Millionaire Journey.

Nick Kovacevich

Nick is a pioneer in the emerging legal cannabis business. This entrepreneur and his partner started Kush Bottles (*www.kushbottles.com*), a packaging and ancillary products distribution company, in 2010. Besides being a competitive athlete, Nick also graduated magna cum laude from Southwest Baptist University. As CEO, he took Kush Bottles public in 2016. Nick became a self-made millionaire at age twenty-seven. One of Nick's Secrets for success is to constantly challenge himself, which is Secret 32 (Challenge Yourself). Nick is quoted in Secret 2 (Define What Success Means to You, Secret 32 (Challenge Yourself), and in First-Hand Advice to Readers Who Are Ready to Begin Their Self-Made Millionaire Journey.

Bunny Lightsey

Bunny and her husband, Rick, co-founded Florida Trophy Gators (*www.floridatrophygators.com*), located in Okeechobee, Florida. They became self-made millionaires in their sixties as a result of being the second of three generations of alligator hunters and processors. A unique enterprise, Bunny and Rick purchase, process, and taxidermy alligators. They place a high value on taking care of others in need. Bunny's words of wisdom are part of Secret 2 (Define What Success Means to You), Secret 10 (Be A Time Master), Secret 41 (Be Grateful), Secret 42 (Place a High Value on Your Personal Life), and Secret 51 (Recognize That It Is Not About the Money.

Connie Lorenz

Connie graduated from a school from which many do not have the right qualifications: the school of hard knocks. She viewed success as having enough money to pay her bills when they came in. While working as secretary/bookkeeper for an asphalt company in Orlando, Florida, she could not understand why a profitable company could not pay its bills. She figured out that the president was embezzling company money. After assisting the out-of-state owner in getting the company back in the black, she was given the company. Connie became a millionaire at age forty-three but did not even know it until she was forty-eight. Her story is part of Secret 9 (Be a Person of Integrity). She is also quoted in Secret 2 (Define What Success Means to You), Secret 10 (Be a Time Master), and First-Hand Advice to Readers Who Are Ready to Begin Their Self-Made Millionaire Journey.

Jeb Lopez

Born in the Philippines, Jeb's dream was to live in the United States. After graduating from college and landing an IT job in Washington, DC, he realized that corporate America was not for him. In 2011 Jeb founded Wheelz Up (*www.wheelzupnow. com*), a business that delivers auto parts to dealers and body and repair shops in the Metro DC area. Jeb became a millionaire at age forty-three. Jeb's words of wisdom are part of Secret 19 (Take Calculated Risks), Secret 42 (Place a High Value on Your Personal Life), and First-Hand Advice to Readers Who Are Ready to Begin Their Self-Made Millionaire Journey.

Gary M.

Gary was the third of seven children born into an Irish Catholic family. He attended Harvard University as a first-generation college graduate in his family and graduated with honors. Besides being recognized as a "Super Lawyer" by *New Jersey Monthly Magazine* since 2005, this civil trial attorney was certified by the New Jersey Supreme Court in 1993. One of Gary's secrets to creating his own success is creating the habit of making friends with all persons. He is quoted in Secret 39 (Be Respectful) and in Secret 51 (Recognize That It Is Not About the Money).

John M.

John was a successful teenage entrepreneur who founded and ran a technology company in the 1990s. He achieved self-made millionaire status when he was seventeen. Years later he worked for two of the largest investment banks before deciding to relocate to Los Angeles to pursue a career in television. John is quoted in Secret 2 (Define What Success Means to You), Secret 4 (Believe in Yourself), Secret 51 (Recognize That It Is Not About the Money), and First-Hand Advice to Readers Who Are Ready to Begin Their Self-Made Millionaire Journey.

Joe Palko

In 1994, Joe and his partner, Scott Sanfilippo, co-founded *www.TheFerretStore.com*, an e-Commerce pet-supply retail company. In 2006, The Ferret Store was sold to Drs. Foster and Smith. Joe became a self-made millionaire at age twenty-five and attributes his success to learning how to be flexible in business. He is quoted in Secret 38 Embrace Change and Secret 51 (Recognize That It Is Not About the Money).

Jason Phillips

Jason is the owner of Phillips Home Improvements (*www.phillipshomeimprovements.com*), a Plano, Texas–based painting and home repair company. This self-made millionaire achieved this status in his thirties and employs more than 150 employees. Pretty good for someone who had $2 left to his name two decades ago. Jason is quoted in Secret 17 (Build a Team), Secret 24 (Pay It Forward), Secret 42 (Place A High Value on Your Personal Life), and Secret 49 (Start a Business).

John Pierce

John is head of recruiting for Stifel, a 125-year-old wealth management firm. John became a self-made millionaire in his forties. One of the secrets to John's success is scheduling time to think.

He is quoted in Secret 2 (Define What Success Means to You), Secret 26 (Take Time to Think), Secret 45 (Create a Financial Roadmap for Yourself), and First-Hand Advice to Readers Who Are Ready to Begin Their Self-Made Millionaire Journey.

Mickey Redwine

This down-to-earth very colorful Texan founded Dynamic Cable Holdings, a company whose three subsidiaries, which he also owns, laid thousands of miles of fiberoptic cable throughout the United States and Mexico.

Even though this Texan Mensch retired in 2002 and had achieved self-made multi-millionaire status in his early thirties, he still works as though his bank account depends on it: by volunteering in unpaid board member positions and other capacities in numerous companies and organizations. Pretty good for a boy who was raised in an impoverished environment, many times with little or nothing to eat. Mickey is quoted in Secret 2 (Define What Success Means to You), Secret 8 (Keep Your Word), Secret 34 (Create Your Own Luck), Secret 42 (Place a High Value on Your Personal Life), and First-Hand Advice to Readers Who Are Ready to Begin Their Self-Made Millionaire Journey.

Dru Riess

Dru is president and CEO of Popular Ink (*www.popular-ink.com*), a McKinney, Texas–based company that employs more than fifty people in a 70,000-square-foot facility that operates twenty-four hours a day, seven days a week. Dru did what it took to get his company off the ground and out of debt after cold-calling on prospects during a five-day car journey around the country and sleeping where he worked, with no insulation or air conditioning. It paid off when he became a self-made millionaire in his twenties. Dru knows what it takes to get the job done. He is also the author of *Sleight of Hand: An Entrepreneur's Bag of Tricks* and is quoted in Secret 10 (Be a Time Master), Secret 35 (Make It Happen), and Secret 45 (Create a Financial Roadmap for Yourself).

Kristen Souza

Kristen and her husband, Joe, have a mission: to spread Aloha through music. They do this by creating the most stunning Hawaiian `ukulele available in the world. They founded Kanile`a `Ukulele (*www.kanileaukulele.com*), based in Kane`ohe, Hawai`i. Kristen became a self-made millionaire in 2007. Together the two are leaders in the ukulele industry with a net worth of $7 million. One of the secrets to Kristen's success is staying focused. She shares the importance of this trait in Secret 12 (Stay Focused).

Allan S.

Allan spent thirty-five years with the New York Philharmonic. He found his first love, playing the violin, at nine years old. Allan became a self-made millionaire in his sixties. He is part of Secret 2 (Define What Success Means to You), Secret 3 (Find Your Passion), Secret 5 (Visualize), Secret 28 (Find a Brain Trust Advisor), and Secret 32 (Challenge Yourself).

Steve S.

Steve spent his career as a successful New York–based attorney. He worked hard to achieve what he valued as important. Steve was dedicated to his profession and provided for his family without compromising his personal standards. His pearls of wisdom are shared in Secret 42 (Place a High Value on Your Personal Life).

Bruce Schindler

Bruce made his first million chasing mammoths. He found his inner passion after graduating from college and moving to Skagway, Alaska.

Bruce (*www.schindlercarvings.com*) carves and restores 35,000-year-old fossilized ivory tusks, which are sold to art galleries and museums. Although raised in an impoverished environment, Bruce's secret to success was spending time with people he saw as role models. Bruce is quoted in Secret 27 (Surround Yourself With People You Want to Be Like), Secret 28 (Find a Brain Trust Advisor), Secret 42 (Place a High Value on Your Personal Life), Secret 49 (Start a Business), Secret 51 (Recognize That It Is Not About the Money), and First-Hand Advice to Readers Who Are Ready to Begin Their Self-Made Millionaire Journey.

Mike Vetter

Mike is the owner of The Car Factory (*www.MTVconcepts.com*), based in Daytona Beach, Florida. His fascination for exotic cars began a world away as he was raised growing up in Germany, Italy, Turkey, and France. He owned his first Lamborghini while still in college, and he has owned and modified just about every car imaginable. Mike became a self-made millionaire at age forty. His strength lies in doing what it takes to get the job done. He is quoted in Secret 2 (Define What Success Means to You), Secret 10 (Be a Time Master), Secret 21 (Persevere), and First-Hand Advice to Readers Who Are Ready to Begin Their Self-Made Millionaire Journey.

James Timothy White

James became a self-made millionaire at age sixteen. At age twelve, he founded his first company in Canada, which he grew into a multi-million-dollar corporate structure. Like many successful entrepreneurs, James experienced bankruptcy. He talked his family into investing in his next venture (*www.wesaysold.com*), which led him to become the world's youngest CEO of a publicly traded company on the Frankfurt Stock Exchange. His strategy for getting people to say yes is featured in Secret 33 (Ask Until You Get a Yes). He is also mentioned in Secret 2 (Define What Success Means to You) and First-Hand Advice to Readers Who Are Ready To Begin Their Self-Made Millionaire Journey.

Brian Wong

Brian is a Canadian-born internet entrepreneur. Raised in Vancouver to parents of Hong Kong/Chinese decent, he graduated high school at age fourteen and college at eighteen. When Brian was nineteen, he launched Kiip (*www.kiip.me*), his own mobile advertising company. He became a self-made millionaire when he was twenty-one, with his business generating $20 million in 2017. One of Brian's strategies for success is surrounding himself with competent staff members. He is quoted in Secret 17 (Build a Team) and Secret 51 (Recognize That It is Not About the Money).

First-Hand Advice to Readers Who Are Ready to Begin Their Self-Made Millionaire Journey

"First, invest in yourself to become great at something. Second, find a job that you are passionate about. Third, be the best at what you do. Fourth, hit a salary goal and invest the rest. And finally, never forget to 'give back.' It will come back to you in ways that you can't measure today." —Rodger D.

"Believe in yourself and don't let anyone tell you that you can't do something because you can, if you really want to!" —Connie L.

"Success comes in many forms; don't put too much weight in your financial success. No amount of money is worth sacrificing the health and happiness of your family, friends, and ultimately yourself. That said, work hard! Be steady in your pursuit of success. Own your shortcomings, own your failures, especially the shortcomings in your own character. Nobody is perfect and not blaming others for your own issues, owning them, leads to living authentically. Your integrity is your greatest asset. Empower

those around you. Don't be afraid of success, don't be ashamed of and limit your own gifts, one of my continuing challenges. Limiting yourself only limits how much you have to give." —Bruce S.

"Never give up, learn how to listen more effectively, learn from defeats, do not be risk averse, and make sure you have some fun along the way!" —John P.

"In all things, always try to be proactive, not reactive. Forward think everything! In life and business, you don't get what you deserve, you get what you negotiate! Sometimes losing means winning. i.e., letting your wife win the argument! It's perfectly fine to aspire to achieve wealth but if you want to achieve happiness as well, find your own balance between the two." —Mickey R.

"Learn how to sacrifice, skip weddings, vacations, outings with friends, become a hermit and focus on your business and sales—the business should always come first. Always sign the checks no matter how big you get, and retain a good attorney who has experience in your industry." —James T.W.

"My advice to anyone beginning their trip to financial freedom is you can absolutely do anything which another person can do. You have all of the same tools as any other self-made millionaire so there is no reason you cannot do the same thing they have done. Surround yourself with people who you want to be like. In my experience you will learn so much from those closest to you and this works both ways so I try to avoid negativity, I try to avoid lazy people, and I always consider the source of advice offered. Someone who is not doing as well as you are is not someone who can offer you helpful advice." —Mike V.

"I say if that's your goal you should reconsider your values. I think you should find what inspires you and go for it. There's no way you can stay committed doing something you don't enjoy even if the money is there." —Chuck C.

"No matter what comes, keep charging forward like a rhino!" —Jeb L.

"You will be on a roller coaster of highs and lows, don't let yourself get too high or too low, and make sure you appreciate every day you are able to learn, grow, and build." —Nick K.

"Pursue a dream—something that excites you and that allows you to exploit your innate talents. Then spend the rest of your life pursuing that dream." —Thomas C.

"Keep gratitude your attitude. If you struggle with this, send yourself simple texts defining what's happening positive each day. The sun is shining today is a great reminder to smile and be grateful." —Laura K.

"Realize that becoming a millionaire will not bring you happiness. Make sure you spend an ample amount of time on your own personal development." —Zach B.

"You must believe in yourself more than anyone else. No matter what age you are or what background you come from no one will champion your pursuits more than you. You must be willing to fail time and time again in order to find the path that leads to a positive result. Become as knowledgeable as possible in whatever field you are trying to make an impact in and never make money be the sole source of motivation. Success can be felt and rewarded on many levels." —John M.

Notes

Introduction

1. Elena Holodny, "The US Is Creating Millionaires Faster Than Anywhere in the World—But It's Not as Impressive as it Sounds," *Business Insider,* November 16, 2017.

2. "Most Millionaires Self-Made, Study Says," *Financial Advisor,* June 13, 2013, *fa-mag.com.*

3. Thomas Stanley, *The Millionaire Next Door* (Taylor Trade Publishing, 1996).

Habit 3

1. Alyssa Pry, "How to Meet Your Money Goals by the End of the Year," Yahoo Finance, October 13, 2017, *https://finance.yahoo.com/news/meet-money-goals-end-year-150953867.html.*

2. Mark McCormack, *What They Don't Teach You at Harvard Business School* (Bantam, 1986).

Habit 6

1. Thomas C. Corley, *Change Your Habits, Change Your Life* (North Loop Books, 2016).

2. Andrew Perrin, "Book Reading 2016," Pew Research Center website, September 1, 2016, *www.pewinternet.org/2016/09/01/book-reading- 2016pi_2016-09- 01_book-reading_a- 01/*.

Habit 7

1. Teresa Bullock Cohen, interview with the author.

Habit 8

1. Billy Epperhart, "How and Why Good Leaders Delegate," *billyeppert.com* blog, July 17, 2017.

Habit 9

1. Ryan Jorden, "What Are the Real Small Business Survival Rates?," *www.linkedin.com,* September 15, 2014.

2. Thomas C. Corley, "How Long Does it Take to Become Rich?," *RichHabits.net,* February 17, 2015.

3. Karin Lenhardt, "29 Valuable Facts About Millionaires," Fact Retriever website, December 27, 2016, *www.factretriever.com/millionaire-facts.*

4. Eden Ryl, "You Pack Your Own Parachute" DVD (Ramic Productions, 1974).

Habit 10

1. Ralph G. Nichols and Leonard A. Stevens, "Listening to People," *Harvard Business Review,* September 1957.

Habit 11

1. Ryan Jaslow, "80 Percent of American Adults Don't Get Recommended Exercise," CBS News, May 3, 2013.

2. Deborah Kotz and Angela Haupt, "7 Mind-Blowing Benefits of Exercise," *U.S. News & World Report* website, March 7, 2012, *https://health.usnews.com/health-news/diet-fitness/slideshows/7-mind-blowing-benefits-of-exercise.*

3. Jack Bosch, "Do You Schedule Time to Think?," *ForeverCash.com,* April 24, 2014.

Habit 12

1. Robert T. Kiyosaki and Sharon Lechter, *Rich Dad's Cashflow Quadrant: Rich Dad's Guide* (Warner Books Edition, 1998).

2. William E. Leuchtenburg, *Franklin D. Roosevelt and the New Deal, 1932–1940* (New York: Harper Colophon Books, 1963), p. 32.

Habit 13

1. Geoffrey James, "How an Upbeat Attitude Makes Success Simple," Inc.com, August 29, 2014, *www.inc.com/geoffrey-james/an-upbeat-attitude-makes-success-simple.html.*

2. Benjamin Hardy, "The Secret to Happiness Is 10 Specific Behaviors," *Observer.com,* July 6, 2015.

3. Yale Middleton, "61 Dominant Serena Williams Quotes," Addicted2Success website, February 10, 2016, *https://addicted2success.com/quotes/61-dominant-serena-williams-quotes/*.

Habit 14

1. Sandra Grauschopf, "Want to Get Lucky? Use These 8 Proven Methods to Boost Your Luck," The Balance website, August 6, 2017, *www.thebalance.com/improve-your-luck-8-ways-to-attract-good-luck-880886*.

Habit 15

1. Christian Trampedach, in reply to "What Is the Percentage of Immigrants to the United States That Make it to Millionaire Status?," Quora website, February 8, 2017, *www.quora.com/What-is-the-percentage-of-immigrants-to-the-United-States-that-make-it-to-millionaire-status*.

Habit 18

1. Scott Wilhite, *The 7 Core Skills of Everyday Happiness* (Whispering Voice Books, 2016).

Habit 20

1. Charles Hamowy, *Financially SECURE Forever* (HCA Consulting, Inc., 2013).

Habit 21

1. "How Does Your Emergency Fund Compare? New Stats Reveal Americans' Rainy Day Savings Habits,"

topinvestor.com, December 29, 2017, *http://topmoney-investor.com/how-does-your-emergency-fund-compare-new-stats-reveal-americans-rainy-day-savings-habits/.*

Habit 22

1. Stan Cho, "More Americans Own Stocks, for Better or for Worse," Nation-Now, February 7, 2018.

2. Barbara Diggs, "5 Ways to Create Passive Income," bankrate.com, July 14, 2017.

3. Sam Walton, *Made in America: My Story* (New York: Doubleday, 1992).

Habit 23

1. Mark Ferguson, "How Do Most Millionaires Make Their Money?," investfourmore.com, September 14, 2015, *https://investfourmore.com/2015/09/14/how-do-most-millionaires-make-their-money/.*

The Secrets for Creating My Own Success That I Have Accomplished

On the following pages, write down the secrets for creating your own success that you have accomplished:

The Secrets That I Will Work on Mastering to Achieve My Self-Made Millionaire Status

On the following pages, write down the secrets that you will work on mastering to achieve your self-made millionaire status:

Other books by Ann Marie Sabath

Business Etiquette In Brief

Beyond Business Casual:
What To Wear To Work If You Want To Get Ahead

Business Etiquette:
101 Ways to Conduct Business With Charm and Savvy

International Business Etiquette—Asia & The Pacific Rim

International Business Etiquette—Europe

International Business Etiquette—Latin America

Courting Business:
101 Ways for Accelerating Business Relationships

One Minute Manners: Quick Solutions to the Most
Awkward Situations You'll Ever Face at Work